The CORRESPONDENCE

of

DAVID COPE & ALLEN GINSBERG

1976–1996

The CORRESPONDENCE

of

DAVID COPE & ALLEN GINSBERG

1976–1996

PDF manuscript copies of David Cope's correspondence
are sources of his works herein, thanks to
The Department of Special Collections, Stanford University Libraries

Original manuscript copies of Allen Ginsberg's correspondence
herein are located in The David Cope Papers,
The University of Michigan Libraries
Special Collections Research Center

GIANT STEPS PRESS
Freeport NY 2020

www.giantstepspress.com

Copyright © 2021 David Cope
Copyright © Allen Ginsberg, used by permission of The Wylie Agency LLC

All rights reserved. No part of this publication may be reproduced or transmitted in any form or by any means, electronic or mechanical, including photocopy, recording, or any information storage and retrieval system, without permission in writing from the publisher, except for brief quotes in reviews.

Thanks to Suzanne Cope, Tim Noakes, Katherine Beam, Rebecca Bizonet, Kathleen Dow, Juli McLoone, Bob Rosenthal, Peter Hale, Jim Cohn, James Ruggia, Andy Clausen, Antler, Sharon Guynup, Steve Miles, Mark Christal, Jon Dambacher, and Christopher Funkhouser.

Cope, David, 1948 –

*The Correspondence of
David Cope & Allen Ginsberg
1976–1996*

ISBN: 9798507617951

Printed in The United States of America.

Front cover photo by Bob Rosenthal © 2021
Back cover author photo by William Cope © 2021
Cover design by Steven Hirsch

Formatting and Technical Consultancy:
Steven Hirsch
(poetsteve@hvc.rr.com)
Emily Rivera
https://emilyrivera846220394.wordpress.com/

First Edition
GIANT STEPS PRESS
GiantStepsPress.com

Works by David Cope

Poetry Books

Quiet Lives, Foreword by Allen Ginsberg. Humana, 1983.

On The Bridge. Humana, 1986.

Fragments from The Stars. Humana, 1990.

Coming Home. Humana, 1993.

Silences for Love. Humana, 1998.

Turn the Wheel. Humana, 2003.

Masks of Six Decades. Nada, 2010.

The Invisible Keys: New and Selected Poems. Ghost Pony, 2017.

A Bridge Across the Pacific: Leaves for Chen Zi'ang, Guan Yin, and Du Fu. Jabber, 2019.

Anthologies (as editor)

Nada Poems. 17 peers. 1988.

Sunflowers & Locomotives: Songs for Allen. Nada, 1998.

Song of the Owashtanong: Grand Rapids Poetry in the 21st Century. Ridgeway, 2013.

Editor and Publisher

Nada Press. *Big Scream.* 1974-2021.

Online

Dave Cope Sampler: http://www.poetspath.com/Dave_Cope/
David Cope Papers at the University of Michigan Special Collections Resource Center:
http://quod.lib.umich.edu/s/sclead/umich-scl-cope?subview=standard;view=reslist

Allen and Dave, 15 March 1983. 67th Street YMCA backstage. Photo by Sharon Guynup.

Table of Contents

Works by David Cope	v
Table of Contents	vii
A Journey of Decades, Burden & Light: Introduction	1
An Allen Ginsberg/David Cope Timeline	5
1976-1979 / Getting to Know You	15
1980-1989: Building a Poetry Life	37
1990-1996: Young Poets for Scream, Beats & Other Rebel Angels, Spring Readings for Gelek Rinpoche	97
CODA: The Intense Finale	117
Appendix A	125
Appendix B	128
Appendix C	129
Appendix D	130
Notes	132
Index Names, Titles, Key Events, Publishers, etc.	147
Related Works	155
About David Cope	157

Friction: Obscure Genius cover photo: David, Antler, Andy Clausen, et al in Allen's 12th Street kitchen.
Photo by Allen Ginsberg, March 15, 1983

A Journey of Decades, Burden & Light: Introduction

by David Cope
2 March 2016

>your kiss disappearing into the night your hand waving
>   pulling away—
>& now, calling each of us before the press releases go out
>   generous gesture even dying
>passing burden & light from Walt thru Williams you & Jack
>   thru those who remain
>   to new nippled generations
>struggling even now to be born.
>
>   —for allen

Allen Ginsberg's *Howl* showed me a path out of seething teenaged rage, and during my college years, I witnessed his October 1969 Moratorium Day reading to 3500 at Hill Auditorium, Ann Arbor. Like so many in that audience, I was brought to tears by his tender and vulnerable reading of *Howl,* which touched both our sorrows and anger at what was happening to the nation in that terrible decade of hopes destroyed, Moloch made visible. I was a young poet, adrift in samsara and yet persistent in recording my poems as I was moved by love or sorrow, the loss of friends, the lies of politicians. Four years later, Allen appeared at the National Poetry Festival in Allendale, not far from my hometown, along with Robert Duncan, the recently reunited objectivist masters Charles Reznikoff, George Oppen and Carl Rakosi, and many others. The message of that conference was to reenvision our former attitudes about our lives, to learn to transcend anger, to build community, and once again I was moved by what he said. I had won two local poetry contests in 1971 and 1972, experimented with many different ways of writing—there were imitations of *Howl,* Dylan Thomas, Duncan, Shakespeare and Chaucer (a "compleynt against clerkes" written while still a student at Michigan) and others, plus the two winning poems from that contest—but I did not yet feel that I had a cohesive vision to share with a master for whom I had enormous respect. Still, I asked him for his address and was given it, along with instructions as to how to get someone to let me in, should I ever be in New York ("holler 'Allen!' from the doorway, and someone will throw the key down to you").

Reznikoff gave me the key to my own initial style—short vignettes, tightly written as in the Chinese masters, yet featuring my co-workers at a spray paint factory in Grand Rapids, friends in our early twenties, weekend apartment cleaning for slumlords, vignettes observed in daily life. These slices of my own life were served up with all the working class suffering and ecstasy that I saw around me, but I also ventured to write similar poems based on the events of the day, paying attention to the "minute particulars" of each tale. I began publishing my *Big Scream* magazine in 1974, and eventually pulled chapbooks together—and here, at last, I thought I might have something worth sharing. I had kept his address, and when I sent him my *Stars* chapbook in March, 1976, he asked for a "dozen copies," and to bill him so that he could send the booklet to "other poets like Snyder and Whalen." I wrote back with a request that he give a copy to Charles Reznikoff, and he wrote me, saying that Charles had died a few months before, recalling an evening where Allen "supped with him in Lincoln Towers middleaged apartments westside Manhattan." So began a correspondence and working relationship, and one of the most profound friendships I have ever known. These letters tell the tale of the changes we—and especially I—went through as we passed two decades as friends: we began with a shared love of Reznikoff and Williams, and he exhibited an enormous patience with me—I was a gifted, but loudmouthed and sometimes tactless kid, still evolving out of an angry teenaged punk, sometimes pretentious when I should have shut up and listened. In some sense, these letters form a kind of bildungsroman, the growth of the young man's mind and the tutelage of a wise elder.

    I think our friendship evolved through his belief in my work, but also our shared love of reading and talking about poets from all over the world and from many ages. I have always been a voracious reader of poetry, whether classics like Dante or Shakespeare or the many varied traditions that came to me through the places where I worked and friends who wanted to turn me on to some new poet I'd not heard of. Once he knew of my desire to publish new and older poets in my *Big Scream* magazine, he also made a habit of sending me many younger poets in need of a venue and a little exposure. In many ways, we were very different from each other: he the famed world traveler, I the mental voyageur working in my garden in Grandville, Michigan, more or less indifferent to travel and sophisticated scenes in big cities, he the gay icon, I the eternally questioning heterosexual with a long-term marriage and raising three kids. Still, we shared lectures and readings, and labored together on ecopoetics and cultural diversity issues, both as college teachers and as builders of programs, and that shared love of the objectivists and old Dr. Williams was a continual light in the friendship.

    After key publications, awards, meeting my peers through his good offices, I grew, and I think he may have as well, through a whole series of shared labors. The end heralded a major change of life for me, with his call on the night of his death, thanking me for our friendship and saying farewell. In the morning he was gone, and while thankful for the many things we shared, I knew that I'd have to reinvent myself yet again. I was not unique in this respect—Allen had many deep friendships, and taught us all to love and respect others whose gifts might be very different from our own, to nourish that light that we could share if we would learn how to overlook each other's failings, to build that sense of community which he nourished in the outrider poets of my generation.

A Few Notes

It is important to give a very special thank-you to Tim Noakes and The Department of Special Collections at the Stanford University Libraries who shared my letters with me via PDF when I wrote with the request. I had known that my letters to Allen were among the correspondence in the Allen Ginsberg Papers there, but had not thought to ask for them, too busy with the details of my own writing career, my exercise and gardening regimens, and the thousand things that fill up a person's life even after end of money-driven worklife. I needed them for a variety of reasons. The larger purpose was to complete a major aspect of my own story found in the letters between us, and to present that in my own archive, The David Cope Papers, which are preserved at the Special Collections Resource Center of my alma mater, The University of Michigan. As a young man, I had kept all of Allen's postcards and letters to me, but did not think to keep my own letters, swept up as I was in larger things than documenting my own journey except in poems. Thankfully, Allen kept them, and as so many of us who knew him have remarked over the years since his death, he remains "the gift that keeps on giving." Indeed, the Stanford collection of my correspondence to Allen includes the largest collection of my poetry manuscripts—both the good poems that Allen championed over the years and those experiments that went awry, as well as some bad poems that make me wince when I see them now.

The initial impetus to ask Stanford for my letters was the publication of Allen's "postcard poem" on page 185 of *Wait Till I'm Dead: Uncollected Poems*. Grove, 2016). That poem was originally published in my *Big Scream* 20, and seeing it in the new book led me to believe that I should retrieve my letters so that I could document my requests to publish it as a poem. Though it was originally prose postcard script, I saw it immediately as an excellent late example of Allen's use of objectivist focus, containing ecological & community health observations, Chinese government thought control bureaucrats, landscape appreciation, older famous man's envy of freer hippies, travelogue & completion of life dream of Han-Shan with Gary Snyder. In the course of working with Stanford's Tim Noakes, Peter Hale of the Allen Ginsberg Trust, Bill Morgan, my friend Jim Cohn, and my curator, Kathleen Dow of the University of Michigan Special Collections Resource Center, I not only retrieved xerograph copies of the letters, but was able to identify one letter by Gregory Corso which was misplaced in Allen's archive. I also learned, in the course of this work, that my Chinese editor and translator, Zhang Ziqing of the Institute of Foreign Literature, Nanjing University, had translated the poem after seeing it in a copy of *Big Scream* 20, and that the translation has been published in his three-volume study of American 20th Century Poetry.

I should end with an enormous note of gratitude to the curators at the University of Michigan's Special Collections Resource Center, especially Katherine L. Beam, who initially contacted me about establishing the archive and curated my work for years before her retirement. Rebecca Bizonet also deserves a huge thanks for her work with me, organizing the materials to develop the first online finding aid for my papers in 2002. Also, a deep thanks to Kathleen Dow, who has been a great friend as the archive grows and changes with the years, and who showed me how to organize my papers from 2002-2013, allowing for the revision and updating of the finding aid and continuing the dialogue on manuscripts and preservation that has at times made me wonder if I missed my calling. Finally, to Juli McLoone, who has been a thoughtful and kind curator. I know that my work is in the best of hands.

George Oppen at National Poetry Festival, 1973. Courtesy of the Grand Rapids Public Library

An Allen Ginsberg/David Cope Timeline

1965   Dave hitchhikes to downtown Grand Rapids and buys *Howl and Other Poems, Kaddish,* and *Reality Sandwiches,* plus *On the Road,* D. T. Suzuki's *Manual of Zen Buddhism* and later, *Dhammapada,* trans. P. Lal.

Oct. 12, 1969   Allen's Pre-Moratorium Reading at Hill Auditorium, Ann Arbor. Featuring a reading of "Howl" to the 3500 people in the audience, including David Cope See description in David's "Congratulations," *Best Minds: A Tribute to Allen Ginsberg.*

June 14-24, 1973 National Poetry Festival at Grand Valley State Colleges, Allendale, Mi. Allen Ginsberg, Kenneth Rexroth, Robert Duncan, Diane di Prima, Charles Reznikoff, George Oppen, Carl Rakosi. David asked for and received Allen's address for later reference.

1974   David founds Nada Press, *Big Scream* magazine, and begins doing small chapbooks via mimeo printing with cover art hand-drawn on mimeo stencils.

1975   Allen's *First Blues: Rags, Ballads & Harmonium Songs* 1971-1974. Full Court Press, 1975.

1975   Allen's *Sad Dust Glories*: poems during work summer in woods. Serendipity, 1975.

1976   David sends his 36 page chapbook, *Stars,* to Allen and receives an enthusiastic response and request for 12 more copies to be sent to poets and editors. Allen to Dave, March 18, 1976 (page 16).

<April 13, 1976: David requests that one copy of *Stars* be sent to Charles Reznikoff and receives a memorable response—note that Charles had died and memento of supping with him in Lincoln Towers, "winter nite stars over the city + cars passing by West side… streets 12 floors below" (page 16).

<Allen begins connecting Dave with publishing opportunities and introductions to other poets, a habit that continues for the rest of his life and which informs many of the initial publication of young poets in *Big Scream*, part of David's desire to build community.

January 25, 1977 The American Airlines letter.   Allen explains Blake's system and writes expansively of his recent reading and teaching. Includes a letter from James Laughlin saying he can't find the copy of David's *Stars*. Allen notes at end of this, "xerox for David Cope," implying that David should send another. David prizes this letter, as it really accelerates the excitement of reading shared by both poets, and while Blake's system was not new to him, he felt that Allen did a superb job of explaining it succinctly (pages 23-26).

Undated letter, early to mid-summer 1977. First mention of the three-in-one book, a compilation edited by Allen and originally featuring Antler, Andy Clausen, and David Cope, to be published by City Lights (page 26). The text shifted to Clausen, Cope, and Bobby Meyers later, and Ferlinghetti eventually felt that he could not publish it. See *I Greet You at the Beginning of a Great Career: The Selected Correspondence of Lawrence Ferlinghetti and Allen Ginsberg, 1955-1997*, pages 235-236, 238, 245-246, 248, 255, Michael Schumacher's *Dharma Lion* (650), and Bill Morgan's *I Celebrate Myself: the Somewhat Private Life of Allen Ginsberg* (523-524). Morgan overstates the case re combining the three poets into one volume; David was not upset about it, as shown in these letters.

1977 David's "Crash" published in *The Pushcart Prize II: Best of the Small Presses*. Ed. Bill Henderson. Yonkers, Pushcart Press, 1977. Nominated by Allen Ginsberg.

1977 *Mind Breaths* published.

March, 1978 First meeting after Allen knew David: his reading in Washington D. C. and party afterward, where he showed me FBI files obtained through FOIA, concentrating on the Ann Arbor and Detroit areas for David's benefit.

1978 Five poems in *City Lights Journal* #4. Ed. Mendes Monsanto. San Francisco: City Lights, 1978. Selected by Allen.

1978 Two poems and "Fragments" in *New Directions* #37. Ed. James Laughlin. New York: New Directions, 1978. One of several poets selected in "Ginsberg's Choice."

1978 Mention of David's 26-page ms. mailed to City Lights, per Allen's request. Possible reference to what would become David's selection for the Three-in-One project. (page 28). See *I Greet You at the Beginning of a Great Career: The Selected Correspondence of Lawrence Ferlinghetti and Allen Ginsberg, 1955-1997*, pages 235-236, 238, 245-246, 248, 255, Michael Schumacher's *Dharma Lion* (650), and Bill Morgan's *I Celebrate Myself: the Somewhat Private Life of Allen Ginsberg* (524).

Sept. 25, 1979 David sketches out difference between his generation and Allen's (pages 32-33).

Feb. 18, 1980 Allen enlists Jim Cohn to help with editing David's manuscript (page 39).

March 1, 1980 Allen writes a recommendation letter to publishers, the first paragraph of which would become the Foreword to *Quiet Lives*, David's first book (page 39).

Summer 1980 First visit to Naropa Institute (now University), Allen's guest: David's reading with Andy Clausen, lectures on Charles Reznikoff and Marsden Hartley.

December 1980 David's letter written after John Lennon's death with unpublished elegy, mention of December 9 reading at University of Michigan Residential College "coffeehouse" (pages 42-44).

January 1981   Allen and David discuss Ferlinghetti's decision not to publish the Three-in-One book (page 45-46).

January 7, 1982 Allen shares David's future publisher Humana Press address, and attaches a copy of his letter to *Time* magazine (December 9, 1981), correcting their misquoting of David's last name as "Pope" in interview (pages 49-50).

1982   *Plutonian Ode: Poems 1977-1980* published.

May 28, 1982   David's misgivings re upcoming Kerouac Conference at Naropa (pages 51-52).

June 21, 1982   David's announcement that he'll come; finances straightened out (page 52).

June 30-July 2, 1982   Jack Kerouac Conference, David as Allen's "honored guest." David reads with Jack Micheline and Peter Orlovsky to an audience of 400 (See note, page 137).

Dec. 1982 The Rimbaud letter from Charleville Allen's letter describing his visit to Charleville "Poetic Holyland" and to the poet's apartment: "how sad his dark old wooden steep stairway, + toilet in his old flat!" One of David's favorite letters from Allen (page 54).

March 15, 1983   pub date of *Quiet Lives* with Allen's Foreword and impromptu book launch and reading with Andy Clausen and Antler, introduced by Allen at the 67th Street YMCA, New York.

May 14, 1983   First mention of David's anthology of poets in his generation, with lineup close to final selection for *Nada Poems*, publ. 1988 (page 55).

March 23, 1984 David's letter noting publication of *Friction 5/6: Obscure Genius* and Randy Roark (see pages 61-62).

November 11, 1984 Allen's "Postcard Poem" from China, later published in *Big Scream* 20, translated by Zhang Ziqing and published in his three-volume study of American 20th Century Poetry, and reprinted as "Poem" in *Wait Till I'm Dead: Uncollected Poems* by Allen Ginsberg. Grove, 2016. (page 63).

1984   Allen's *Collected Poems 1947-1980*. New York: Harper & Row, 1984.

1985   Allen's "Dear David: hazy in steamer lounge" (postcard poem) published in *Big Scream 20* (page 65).

Feb. 1985   David thanks Allen for letting him sit with him as he signs copies of his *Collected Poems* at the Detroit Institute of Art (page 65).

Apr. 14, 1986   David writes re his upcoming visit to read in Andy Clausen's series, Boulder (pages 69-70).

Apr. 18, 1986   Allen replies re Boulder visit and says "tell Humana to send new book to Amer. Academy," likely his first prompt toward American Academy, later awarded to *On the Bridge* (page 70).

Aug. 24 1986   *On the Bridge*, David's second book to be published. See David's letter of Aug. 24, 1986 for first ref. (page 72)

1986   Allen's "It's All So Brief" and "No Longer" published in *Big Scream* 21.

1986   *White Shroud: Poems 1980-1985*. New York: Harper & Row, 1986. David noted reception of signed copy Feb. 3, 1987 (page 73).

1986   *Howl: Annotated*. Ed. Barry Miles. New York: Harper & Row, 1986.

1986   Allen's "Cadillac Squawk" published in *Big Scream* 23.

Feb. 4, 1987   Allen received *On the Bridge* (page 73).

March 31, 1987 David received signed copy of *Howl: Annotated*. Letter also features preview of Summer 1987 Objectivist Conference at Naropa Institute (now University) and request for Allen's early essay, "Poetry, Violence, and the Trembling Lambs" for upcoming issue of *Big Scream* (page 74).

June 12, 1987   David sends exact set of Rakosi poems prepped for set he and Allen will share at the Naropa Objectivist Conference (pages 74-75).

July 1987   Objectivist Conference at Naropa Institute (now University). Allen Ginsberg, Carl Rakosi, Marie Syrkin, David Cope, others.

Undated, 1987   High-spirited postcard to David from Allen, Chris Ide and Chris Funkhouser (pages 76-77).

1987   Allen's essay, "Poetry, Violence, and the Trembling Lambs" reprinted in *Big Scream* 24.

Oct. 30 1987   David confirms his visit to Brooklyn College in Allen's series, with topic suggestions (pages 77-78).

March, 1988   David's Brooklyn College/NYC visit and reading, with Eliot Katz, others.

March 25, 1988   Lineup and plans for publication of *Nada Poems* after receiving news that David had won the American Academy and Institute of Arts & Letters award in literature (award not mentioned here, but implicit with plan to publish larger print run) (page 81).

Sept 12, 1988   David sends 2 proposed lineups for Naropa eco-conference he had suggested earlier to Anne Waldman. David did major prep work for the conference, including first draft of what became the conference document, "The Declaration of Interdependence" (pages 82-89).

Jan. 30, 1989   David to Allen and Bob Rosenthal, preliminary publicity requests for Allen's and my reading at Grand Valley State University, Grand Rapids, Mi. (pages 87-89).

Apr. 20, 1989   Allen and David read at Grand Valley State University, Grand Rapids.

1989-1990   Allen's "I Went to the Movie of Life" published in *Big Scream* 27.

1990   David's *Fragments from the Stars* published.

Summer, 1990   Ecology and Poetics Conference, Naropa Institute (now University). With Allen, Gary Snyder, David, Antler, Peter Warshall, Bill DeVall, others. Included four days of editing the draft of "A Declaration of Interdependence" originally drafted by David. Final evening before presentation spent with Allen, going over the document together; presentation to the press on the final day of the Conference. The document was later published in *Disembodied Poetics: Annals of the Jack Kerouac School.* Ed. Anne Waldman and Andrew Schelling. U of New Mexico Press, 1994. (Page 466, with acknowledgement of David's role, page X). See also July 14, 1990 letter to Bob Rosenthal for brief description of the conference.

Feb 19, 1993   Allen reads and lectures at GRCC, introduced by David.

<*Thanks*, brief chapbook of poems by David and students at Grand Rapids Community College, a thank-you gift for Allen's reading and lecture at the college.

Feb 19-20, 1993 Collaborative document. Summary of Allen's lectures written by Cope from his notes taken in auditorium, edited by Allen and revised. Later published in *A Poet's Sourcebook,* course booklet for David's Creative Writing classes, Grand Rapids Community College. 3 successive editions (pages 104-106).

July 28, 1993   David sends Allen preliminary copy of his multicultural literature sourcebook (text) for his class, ed. David Cope. Grand Rapids Community College, two editions (page 108).

1993   Allen's "American Sentences" and "In The Benjo," in *Big Scream* 32 (1993). Allen Ginsberg cover photo by Darlene Kazmarczyk.

1993   David's *Coming Home* published. Totowa: Humana, 1993. Includes "White Light," paean to the friendship with Allen."

Undated, likely Jan. 1994 David asks to spend time with Allen after his first Hill Auditorium reading for Jewel Heart Buddhist Community /The University of Michigan (pages 108-109).

Feb. 4, 1994   First Jewel Heart / University of Michigan Reading, with "Howl" as featured poem.

April 10, 1994   David's request for "The Big Parade" for *Allen Ginsberg: Shared Dreams, Some Roots & Later Leaves, Some Sources & Descendants.* Ed. David Cope. Grandville: Nada, 1994. (Page 110).

May 23, 1994.   Allen's instructions to his office staff re completion of recommendation for David's entry into PhD program, using Foreword to *Quiet Lives* as opening paragraph and adding script in this letter as second (page 110).

<u>July 1994   Beats and Other Rebel Angels Conference</u> Naropa Institute (now University). Featuring Allen and other living Beat writers, plus a cadre of young poets. David read with Galway Kinnell, Sharon Olds, and Ed Sanders at Boulder High School.

July, 1994   *Allen Ginsberg: Shared Dreams, Some Roots & Later Leaves, Some Sources & Descendants.* Ed. David Cope. Grandville: Nada, 1994. Course pack for my class in Allen's later poems at the Beats & Other Rebel Angels Conference, Naropa 1994.

July 21, 1994   David's note of thanks for Allen's compassion to Karen Ide after her son Chris's funeral (page 111).

Feb. 1995   Second Jewel Heart / University of Michigan Reading, with "Kaddish" as featured poem.

17 Feb. 1995   David's responses to Allen's concern about being overwhelmed reading "Kaddish" (page 112).

1995   *Cosmopolitan Greetings*: 1986-1992. New York: HarperCollins, 1995.

1996   Allen's "After Europe! Europe!" and "The Bonfire (Rescued at the Last Minute)," in *Big Scream* 34 (1996). Poems from 1958 and 1957, respectively.

Spring 1996   Third Jewel Heart / University of Michigan Reading, with new poems featured.

Apr. 7, 1996   David's responses to Allen's reading (page 112).

Apr. 5, 1997   Allen's death.

May, 1997 "Closing the Bardo" ceremony, readings, and performances in place of Fourth Jewel Heart / University of Michigan Reading, including Gelek Rinpoche, Gyuto Monks, Anne Waldman, Patti Smith, Natalie Merchant, Bob Rosenthal and David, among others.

25 May 1997 Coda letter to Jim Cohn with extensive description of the previous "Closing the Bardo" Ceremony (pages 118-120).

1997 *Sunflowers & Locomotives: Songs for Allen.* Cover photo of Allen on 12th St. fire escape by Christopher Funkhouser, back cover photo of Allen and Peter Hale by Steve Miles. Mementos, elegies and paeans for Allen after his death, including work by Carl Rakosi, Lawrence Ferlinghetti, Gary Snyder, Diane di Prima, Anne Waldman, Andy Clausen, David and many others. Includes xerox of Allen's handwritten lyrics and arrangement of Blake's "Nurse's Song" (published 1997).

1998   David's *Silences for Love* published. Totowa: Humana, 1998. Dedication for Allen ("Calm Sea Clear Shore"), this volume includes elegy "for allen" on pages 116-117.

19 July 1998   David to Jim Cohn, on return to Naropa a year after Allen's death— "what I learned" (pages 120-123)

2003   David's *Turn the Wheel* published. Totowa: Humana, 2003. Includes the following elegies for Allen: "Lost Loves" (4) and "Yeah, an' here he was" (26-27), obliquely as the "one-eyed bard" in "the dharma at last" (48-49), and memorialized with Chris Ide in "Madadeyo in Dreams" (80-81).

Charles Reznikoff among students and poets. National Poetry Festival, 1973.
Courtesy Grand Rapids Public Library.

Robert Duncan, Charles Reznikoff, George Oppen and Carl Rakosi photo from National Poetry Festival, Allendale, Mi. 1973. Courtesy of Grand Rapids Public Library.

Carl Rakosi at National Poetry Festival, 1973. Courtesy of the Grand Rapids Public Library

1976-1979 / Getting to Know You

Allen Ginsberg at National Poetry Festival, Allendale, Mi. 1973. Courtesy of Grand Rapids Public Library.

Allen to David   March 18, 1976

      Dear David Cope: I enjoyed *The Stars* you sent: clear observation, humble or straightforward attitude toward ordinary reality, spaciousness of view from asphalt under yr feet up to the sky turning blue & good humored appreciation of your own sanity. "Staring blankly … empty city" …*Baseball*, "old woman highway home coffee," "fisherman jerks…white belly" …*Crash* "hands in pockets" …Lavender sky, *Three Fields* tractor deer tracks mixed, *Dreaming on you* —in fact just about every poem had real neat solid realistic "ordinary-mind-romantic-realistic lines… "these things are enough this morn." Yes. You're so smart! and right! Some remind me of my own *Empty Mirror*. Send me a dozen copies, bill me, & I'll send yr *Stars* to other poets like Snyder & Whalen. Thank you—Allen Ginsberg.

      [side bar] I don't often receive poem books readable as yours.

David to Allen   undated, between March 18-April 13, 1976
                                                                                                      via Reznikoff request

Dear Allen

      Thank-you for your kind note about my *Stars,* & for your book *Sad Dust Glories*. I have enclosed the 12 copies you requested & feel that your giving them to friends is more than adequate payment for them, therefore no bill. Will also send *Big Scream* when it comes out next. Thanks again.

                                            Dave Cope

PS If you could get a copy of *Stars* to Charles Reznikoff I would deeply appreciate it. I have always stood in awe of his work & would like to think of him having a copy of mine. DC

                          [in Allen's hand: Nada Press
                                         696 48th St S E
                                         Grand Rapids Mich]

Allen to David   Paterson NJ April 13, 76

Ah David Cope

      Alas Reznikoff died about 2 months ago—82 years old. I'd supped with him in Lincoln Towers middleaged apartments Westside Manhattan a few months ago—January—winter nite stars over the city + cars passing by West Side dark streets 12 floors below. I read your poems—parts side by side w/ Reznikoff's texts as sample of clear eyed method—Black Sparrow has vol. I Complete Rez work now out.

      Look me up if our paths ever cross—

                                           Allen Ginsberg

Thanks for the books. I'll send them to Ferlinghetti, Creeley, Rakosi, Laughlin + Bunting etc. & Dylan. Enclosed $12 for token costs.

[Sidebar] PS. Please send me any later publications—It was such a pleasure to look thru yr clear skull in *Stars*

Allen to David [left sidebar] August 28, 1976

David: I re-read *The Stars* & still am tickled by your simplicity + precision— "*Big Scream*" [,] "Rain," "Party's canoeing, "The Ball Game," "Waking Together" 1 of 3, + "The Wind" esp. #3 sustain your clear mind's articulations.

I know some other young poets whose imagistic realism you might like—are you looking for matter for *Big Scream* [Cope's magazine], or interested in checking out other folks' stirrings

The rest of the work in *Scream* was also readable. How old are you what do you do for money? any new booklets? I sent yr *Stars* to James Laughlin, 333 6th Ave N. Y. who appreciated it—as well as to Rakosi + a few others. Send me more copies of *The Stars*, if you have them.
Love, Allen Ginsberg.

David to Allen Sept 14, 1976

Dear Allen

I started to write you a letter, which became a section of long poem I am currently writing. This section, enclosed, contains most of what you wanted to know. I want to thank you again for your continued encouragement & will stay in touch. *Big Scream* 8 in October.

Dave [Cope]

PS: the 2 postcards you've sent contain 2 of the loveliest poems I've seen. If you have others, I'd love to see them. Also did you send *Attaboy*? A friend of mine Jim McCurry is in there too—

Attachment: "Dear Allen," 2 ½ pages of autobiographical poem explaining myself to Allen, later abandoned.

David to Allen Oct. 1, 1976

Dear Allen

Thinking it over, perhaps my last letter to you wasn't clear in some respects—

1. I have no money & publish on a shoestring. The largest edition of *Big Scream* was 150 copies; *The Stars*, 100.
2. I am interested in any poems sent in mail to me—whoever you may have in mind is welcome to submit—I would be interested in shorter poems of yours; if you wouldn't mind a small, non-literary but attentive audience. Many of my readers are blue-collar workers who wouldn't give a shit about reading anything else except maybe *High Times* or *Rolling Stone*; dope dealers, etc. While I am peripherally curious about the literary scene, frankly what I've seen of it

scares the hell out of me; except when making a friend & following their progress along with mine; such as Jim McCurry in Denver or Michael McMahon in Maine.

Therefore I've opted for a non-committal approach to the literary world—not knowing how to enter the door without enduring the cackles & the snorting—maybe I'm naïve? I'd love to make some friends tho—that's where I'm at.

Dave Cope

Allen to David October 8, 1976

Dear David Cope
Thanks for the clear poem + letters. Back from Berlin + Paris, I brought *The Stars* & read half of it to Gregory Corso, who asked me to send him a copy, which am doing, of the 5 new ones you sent me. It's a good book; I sent one to Oppen also who read + liked it. I didn't mean to plunge you into Baudelariain Bohemia. It's just that I've seen clear + lovely work by about 10 poets in recent years, a surprising harvest, some kinda wave of new clarity + charm + energy—from diverse [illegible] such as yrself. Thanks for mind photos. —Allen Ginsberg.

[right sidebar] I meditate on this empty sky-colored image of Buddha.

David to Allen Nov./Dec. 1976

Dear Allen
Sorry about the delay between letters; I've been working on *Big Scream* 8, which I hope you've gotten by now. The UPS situation on the east coast has really screwed up my mailings—& your last postcard, with the lovely blue Buddha, arrived a month after you sent it too. It's a shame no one in the art publishing business has thought to put out a large book of Indian paintings—what I've seen of it, the lavish colors & the elaborate schema of the pictures could have a salutary effect on western art.
I have a few questions if you've got time—how does one go about touring & reading one's work? Is there much money in it? I'm at a peculiar impasse right now, in that if I could raise some money, I could greatly expand my publishing—& I feel now that that's what I want to do.
Have you seen the article on !Kung tribesmen in December *Psychology Today*? Seems to me an application of rock & roll for healing, supposing a concert could go on all night.
Also I'd like to send *Big Screams* to Robert Creeley—do you think he'd be interested & if so could I have his address?
Guess that's all for now. Things are snowy & romantic in G.R. & I'm sure New York is the same.

Love
Dave Cope

Attachment: handwritten five line untitled poem, abandoned.

18

Allen to David   Dec. 10, 1976

Dear David Cope
    Please send along w./ enclosed note copies of *Big Scream* #3 + your *Stars* to poet/editor Harvey Shapiro at *N.Y. Times*. The note's self-explanatory. That's one way of getting money.
    Touring + reading is a lot of work and I can't explain in letter how to do it—requires activity publishing, or accident, etc.
    Try to send work to Lewis McAdams S.F. State College Poetry Center, S.F. Calif, and to Ann Waldman at Naropa Institute re St. Mark's in N.Y.C. But nobody has money for fare that distance.
    If there's any school around Grand Rapids that would be willing to pay me my "standard" fee of $1,500 (or $1000 bargain price) + fare, I'd be glad to give a reading with you + leave you with half the fee. That should pay for some printing. I'll probably be out reading / touring this Spring. (I'd have to check dates with my agent Charles Rothschild 330 E. 48 St N.Y.C. 10017 212- PL 287533). Our manila enveloped letters crossed in the mail. Have you applied for Government Grants? Or [illegible] National Endowment? C.C.L.M etc? You can get information also from Poets + Writers, 201 W54th St. N.Y. 212-PL-71766 "Directory of Amer Poets" gives schools that have readings.
    At this point I can't exactly tell you "how to" though I'd be glad to read with you if you can arrange any readings using me as bait.

                                      Ah
                                      Allen G.

If you could xerox a complete mss. of a book of poems by you all prepared, I'd be willing to show it to whatever publishers I run across. I'm too overloaded with work to be efficient but by accident something might come of it.

    Re Creeley
    400 Fargo
    Buffalo N.Y. 14213
    716-886-0475
    Anyone you write to, you're welcome to use my name to say I encouraged you to write, or suggested, etc.

David to Allen: Missing letter sent with copy of my *Go* chapbook.

Allen to David   Jan 3, 1977

Dear David Cope
    Received your booklet *Go* today & read it, some firmness I've always liked in most poems and many many lines throughout the pages—as I keep saying it's always a pleasure to read your words because you're always (almost) saying something clear about something clearly seen. I keep thinking there must be something I can or shd do to circulate your work or try to help you

get a book published. Harder to arrange readings for $ without a book to circulate. I forgot, but I think I wrote you about this; I will try to get St. Mark's Church Poetry Project to sponsor a reading and will work on what I can via Naropa Institute next summer.

"frozen wind rips at our ears" rips is terrific.

"Where there's sorrow let me be there" poem Reznikoff [written for memory of C.R.] is sharp & clear and heartfelt. Labor Day funeral cortege "the women covering their faces" is visible. The poem maybe the most consistently transparent, clear. "Just another face among so many" —OK even sorta coincident w/ Buddhist view. 60's war recollections are fine! Did you try the *NY Times*???

"faces chew rolls…racing thru heavy traffic…Big dipper above trees" are definite

Birth's a well told story.

The Farm's solid—reminds me of my own Eclogue.

The Field has concentrations as in a single moment of old Haiku. Terrific swiftness like yr near simultaneous sun burst & shotgun blast. I really do appreciate your alertness & precision…I mean yr alertness & precision is appreciable by others, you make yr perceptions so evident.

TV snowstorm's accurate decade summary again.

from "hospital corridors" to velvet lavenders of paradise (like your "telephone poles silhouetted against lavender sky") to bleak Orion straddling sky, that last poem is an interesting attempt to make a complete cycle of "ordinary mind" vasty vision—real interesting condensation. —Thanks—

Allen

[Sidebar:] Did I send your recent pamphlet old letters to Eberhart? If not I'll send one. A.G.

Allen to David Jan. 14, 1977

Dear David Cope:

Thanks for new *Big Scream*—always interested to see yr progress report on the history of your space & your head in it—I think a lot of people are wondering how they "put the violence behind me." Calm wakening all thru this set of poems, curiosity about the tangled nets everyone is in—& lots of nice details! (faces, [illegible] and all [illegible]).

Oddly possible as you know, but also "Peace" + the others would seem [appropriate] on the op ed pages, if anyone had energy [illegible] & push yr texts there. I keep feeling I ought to try, then think no it's (yr work) too delicious exactly as it is calm by itself (and anyway I'm a vicious busybody).

All David Montgomery's short prose pieces were solid and full of real detail, I liked them.

I'm enclosing a book from a friend I haven't seen in years, but like his book—different style than yours but very live and generous—Andy Clausen.

Yours
Allen Ginsberg

P.S. Please keep sending me what you print [address follows]

Attachment: "The Rose."

David to Allen   Jan. 1977

Dear Allen

I'm bursting with a million things to say, questions, etc. First, I could arrange to spend a week or a few days in New York this summer, if St. Mark's Project could give me a hand. My sister lived there 3 years, & I have an outlander's bedazzled love of the city. The idea of reading there is really appealing to me.

You've mentioned on a few occasions my work is usually clear—could you show me areas to work on, your perspective would help me sift lines. Am enclosing 2 more poems for the *GO* set—I worry that, being over-eager, I might be pushing my work on you too fast. When I get excited, I turn things out like a madman.

The latest postcard, L'Allegro, is incredible—I haven't seen it before. We have a set of Blake cards from Tate Museum. Curious [that] the genitals should be obscured <also true of Satan in *Job*, maybe a link, but perhaps that was the time in which he lived. I wonder what you're reading now; presently I'm going thru Baudelaire's *Fleurs de Mal*, ND, thinking there must be a better translation than this. Tried translating "Comes the Charming Evening" & again have had to conclude a rough adaptation would be clearer & more energetic. Also reading Duncan's *Roots & Branches*—his "Two Dicta of William Blake" is a favorite of mine. A public reading by Duncan is my idea of heaven.

I enjoyed Andy Clausen's book—he tends at times to be a little too topical/political for me—I'm not sure which word fits—but he has a free-swinging way with phrasings that I appreciate. Have you seen much by Jim McCurry? His *Machine 1.12* will be out soon; maybe I can get you a copy. His work, mostly prose, has a neat American madness/hit the road again sense, as I got from Kerouac, especially thinking of all the jobs & scenes in *On the Road*.

About your suggestion—I've written Grand Valley College about your possibly reading there sometime in spring, mentioned terms & will get back to your agent if anything turns up.

Guess that's all for now—thanks for Creeley's address—I'll keep in touch

Dave

PS Thanks again for everything you've done to encourage me. I sent "Peace" to *NY Times*. Also, please send your pamphlet (old letters to Eberhart). I haven't seen it.

David to Allen   In Allen's hand: David Cope w/McCurry's prose Jan 13, 77

Dear Allen

This mostly in response to your letter, exploding with energy. Haven't read much aloud lately, other than Chaucer, whom I do monthly—I understand Blake's system but haven't felt ready to plunge through "Jerusalem" or "Milton," read them twice in my early twenties. Perhaps should try them again, certainly I could read 'em if I had somebody to read with. I've usually been drawn to the shorter works, or "Urizen" or "Los," "Marriage of H & H." "The Sick Rose," "Ah Sunflower," prophecies. I've also spent odd hours—years ago, on LSD, correlating Blake, Kabbalah, & "mystical" systems, all of which I found similar. *Tibetan Bk of the Dead* ecstatic visions,

>   The starry floor,
>   The watry shore
>   Is giv'n thee till the break of day.

I am no mystic, in full blown sense, but have always felt surrounded by voices, authors—someone; protected by wolf god & coyote, also St. Francis of Assisi, St. Christopher—tho I'm no Catholic. I do know things at first hand.

Have read 1 + 2 *Paradise Lost* to Sue aloud—I can really get into various voices of devils, whiny Belial & big brutish bass Moloch, etc. Milton's lines have a funny garbled effect on me:

>   Of man's first disobedience / and the fruit
>   (here, snapping the line in two)

I don't know fancy metrics, can't be specific—his choice of latinate terms, perhaps; but you oughta hear me read Chaucer! I know French, Spanish, & Latin from high school, doing Baudelaire from original, dissatisfied with translations I've seen & I think I could do better, in a free way. I don't think Chaucer can be read without knowledge of French, so much of his language is French.

Of older writers I am fondest of Petronius & Catullus; the unvarnished truth in them, & tho the sarcasm occasionally gets in the way, I like the adventure & the craziness. Of Greeks, Aristophanes is the only dramatist for me; & both of Homer's books.

When we get together some time I'd love to read aloud back & forth, recalling you & Reznikoff & Enslin trading off Finnish poems "O do not sing me into a fen" at Poetry Festival here a few years ago is a warm memory.

Other news—I won Pushcart Prize, among 3000 entrants, & want to thank you again for submitting my book—winning poem was "Crash," which surprised me, in a way. No word from Harvey Shapiro—I sent the letter to zip 10036, amazed that your & my correspondence is so quick, imagining incredible warehouses of mail in New York. I'm almost done with Michael McMahon's book, stylistically a funny cross between Robert Frost & Robert Bly—sometimes Mike's work leans a little too heavily on Bly's sort of imagery & transitions for me, but he has a grip on silence that carries me off.

Jim McCurry's *Machine* with this letter, 2 segments.

I'm reading *Paterson* now—I go back to it a lot. Read Spenser Bk 1 The Redcross Knight years ago & enjoyed it as a multifaceted jewel, the elegant rhythms & the elaborate allegory—tho it hasn't stayed with me as a favorite. Shakespeare—I go most often to *Lear, Macbeth*; & *Henry IV.1* is a favorite because it's so funny; "whoreson mad dog," "stuffed cloakbag of guts"—for years my friends & I greeted each other with these, not at all poetic perhaps but a crazy good time. I'm as fond of a good curse as any plumber or factory rat.

Wrote Andy Clausen & sent B.S. 8 with invitation to be in #9. I'm wondering if I ought to send you a few previous incarnations—from 1974 to 1975, up to *Stars,* I published 6 *Big Screams*, uneven quality, as I was still trying to figure out what I wanted to do, but they are energetic, with definite high points by authors Montgomery, Greinke—Greinke has done an excellent adaptation/translation of some of Rimbaud, very readable, William Harrold, various metamorphoses of my work, & my wife Susan's whimsical short work, disarming & often straight to the heart: she is one of Andy Clausen's derelict women poets.

    About all for now—I'm so happy we can talk about the old poets—so often I've wanted to open up about them, & had writers look at me as if to say, "whaddya bother with that old shit for?", which irritated but also confused me; I'm in love with the old folks, & feel I can never stop learning from them. I'll keep in touch.

Dave

PS: nothing from Grand Valley yet. Do you ever read Whitman aloud?

Return envelope & postage enclosed for McCurry's ms.—I'll be publishing "Devil's Notebook" in B. S. 9. If you have anything up to 8 pages, I'd love to publish it; sometime this summer: Mag would include you, me, McCurry, & Andy Clausen if he sends things, maybe Montgomery, who is my oldest friend in writing.

PPS: reading "Jerusalem"—

> In Selfhood, we are nothing: but fade away in morning's breath.
> Our mildness is nothing: the greatest mildness we can use
> Is inescapable & nothing! None but the Lamb of God can heal
> This dread disease: none but Jesus! O Lord descend and save!

> Flat on the ground, & yet I'm floating!

Allen to David   **American Airlines**
                            In Flight   Jan 25, 77
                            Altitude   over U.S.A.

Dear David:
    Flying for half week Buddhist meditation $ benefit UCLA and a niteclub act at Café Troubadour 2 nites w/ musicians singing Blake+ Blues & reading new poems.

    I just spent 2 weeks in Baltimore woodshedding with 18 year old poet friend both of us reading 6-10 hours a day from beginning to end the Complete Poetry & Prose of William Blake. I'm up to the last mature porphyry-voiced pages of *Jerusalem* and it's led my mind thru inspired changes. Blake's system is not hard to understand if you read his work from beginning to end, and as it got clearer it seemed a sublime investigation + his Ambition + creation greater than any other literary poet—Jerusalem's pure gold mind & poesy & voice. Erdman's big paperback complete illustrated illuminated books in black + white, + Bloom's notes at back of Erdman—Bloom Complete text + Keynes' paperback oxford complete works in chronological order (tho over-punctuated) + S. Foster Damon's paperback *Blake Dictionary* are the 4 books you need to penetrate the whole panorama + locate all the characters + their symbolic function. It <u>all</u> boils down to 4 Principles (Zoas) [:] <u>Reason</u> (Urizen) <u>Imagination</u> (Urthona + Los) <u>Body</u> (Tharmas) and <u>Emotions</u> (Luvah) trying to dominate each other, going out of synch, thus becoming "spectres" of themselves by getting cut off from their "Emanations" or projections of feminine sympathy. So all the prophetic books are Blake's vision of them in Combat, using personal + contemporary history for scenes & exaggerating the themes in cosmic-large humor, and describing all the disrelations + their psychological consequences + historical unfoldings till the prophesied whole man "Albion" be reunited with his emanation "Jerusalem" + all four, Reason, Imagination, Emotion, + Body cooperate democratically. That's the basic theme, worked out in delicate detail—

> "Labor well the minute particulars, attend to the Little Ones:
> And those who are in misery cannot remain so long
> If we do but our duty: labor well the teeming Earth" –

Jerusalem plate 55 1. 51-53

Reading all that inspired me to write 25 page long line blakean poem with 2 characters [,] old letcherous [sic] bard + young chaste messenger in Poetic-erotic contest, a sort of autobiographical play-out of my own projections in symbolic form, fertile way, I never did that before—or not since 1950.

I read aloud most of *Paradise Lost* (first time I read it thru) late last year also—that helped get a fix on Blake, both his sound and his revision of Biblic-Miltonic symbolism. I think I'll go on this year + read all Shelley chronologically, & *Fairy Queen* of Spencer, & Byron & Wordsworth's *Prelude + Excursion*, etc. things I put off impatient but now I'm fifty and those works are fascinating to me for the first time. Epic poetry's not impossible to create now. Also in Baltimore read Shakespeare's Sonnets thru (relating to my own love themes) & Poe's poetry while visiting his grave & tiny brick house—great rhythm + really interesting aesthetic of Beauty, some actual Eidolon not to be despised, tho obsessive.

All last year I read + taught Williams, Reznikoff, & associated naturalist-imagists Marsden Hartley's poems Dig those! rare book, Holt 1945 (?); Lawrence's poems, Kerouac poems; some Rakosi; Blythe's 4 vols. Haiku—and for Naropa classes taught + sang Elizabethan ballads + Campion + Nash lyrics out of various standard anthologies —and lots of Wordsworth + Shelley standard pieces with my dying father—who said of W.W.'s Immortality's "…we come from God who is our home" "that's beautiful, but it's not true." I also read him Bryant's *Thanatopsis* which he'd always taught in high school-a little motheaten but not bad mood. This kid poet friend is an imperious maniac reader who keeps pushing me to read poesy + stop being a poetry businessman. So we went off together to read Blake—& every few days in Johns Hopkins library consulted the Trianon Press facsimile editions of Blake's colored plates of each book—all available now in libraries. If you've never seen his Jerusalem in printed facsimile you've got a sublime brilliant surprise for your eyeballs to eat. Odd you asked me what I've been reading of late because I've been really immersed in prophetic readings, just came home yesterday, + flying off today with Collected Blake to finish over L.A. on jetplane before I land.

Yes keep sending me poems, they always are a satisfaction to read + sustain my pleasure at knowing your mind + eyes + presence. If I'm slow at answering don't mind I get into busy jags—now isolate on plane there's some time.

I'll be in Naropa Boulder June 1 to Aug 23—there is plenty room in my apartment you can stay at all you like, use my room. Peter Orlovsky will be at Naropa probably, so the house will be almost empty—his girlfriend Denise Felieu will be there in and out—address is 437 E 12 st. Apt. 23, no bell downstairs, yell up at front window or phone from around the corner 212-777-6786.

Larry Fagin + others Rochelle Kraut [inserted after others] who work at St. Marks live in the same building. I think they are trying to arrange some reading for you at St. Marks—Larry has your books—maybe I'll be able to find out more when I return early January. In any case you have a place to stay + eat here. The apt. is between Ave. A + First Ave, 3 blocks from St. Marks Church—where I'll read with Robert Lowell Jan 23. Or pass by Naropa Boulder in Summer. I once read a lot of Baudelaire + my Angel kid has read every translation—apparently, if you don't know French (I do) you have to read all the translations to get a good idea. Penguin might have a prose tr. Duncan's *Opening of the Field* turned me on, as a leaved book, esp his line of Pindar poem referring to Whitman. I'll be reading with Duncan April 7 in Colorado, after 2 weeks teaching at Naropa Boulder. I love Clausen's phrasings—

> "I had just come back
> from the enemy must be killed" etc.

And some of his extravagant-realistic conceptions like "the derelict women poets are coming," it's a great humor often really intelligent + surprisingly individual, original self-mind. The poem about "The Star" is great, as story + phrasing—quite serious + sad, I've cried over its truthfulness, reading it to sneering dumb untruthful students sometimes. Clausen's "dumb" but he's a dumb genius in a way, with godly insights—his compassion's real— "are they death's children?"—the bums he means. His domestic idealism is unusual and delightful.

Any answer from Harvey Shapiro *N.Y. Times*? New "Rose" equally good as others in *Go* book [Cope's chapbook after *Stars*]—you ask for criticism. The first section's o.k. but not as true in detail as marvelous dreamed stream—because the generalizations aren't nailed down enuf— "prophesies of doom" [illegible] no more gas or protein crisis or greenhouse effect smog maybe— some specific doom— "robot politicians" isn't gleaming enough lacking more grisly specificity— "attend to the little ones." From a thousand Turks buried alive thru Israel it gets better into more accurate therefore funny-serious focus. So 4 lines— "prophesies of doom" "angry governors etc" "population doubles, etc" and "wars + rumors etc" could be enlivened as the Turks + cows are more live. For the rest it's almost totally delicate. "Production number" that one line is a little weaker than the rest of that section which ends solid + specific in its lines. OK. See you sooner or later—Best wishes—Allen (Ginsberg).

Attachment: Copy of James Laughlin's letter to Allen re my *Stars*, which Allen sent to him.

New Directions Publishing Corporation
333 Sixth Avenue
New York City 10014

AL 5-0230 Cable: Newbooks
June 7, 1977

Mr. Allen Ginsberg
c/o Naropa Institute
1111 Pearl Street
Boulder, Colorado 80302

Dear Allen:

Many thanks for your letter written from City Lights not long ago.

I don't mind if the sequence of poems about your father appears in Ferlinghetti's book before our annual. It would be of significance to me to use those poems about your father because I liked him so much.

I wonder if I ever received the pamphlet from David Cope. The poetry books are all pretty well alphabetized, and it doesn't turn up where it should, if I had it.

[sidebar, in Allen's hand:] Tell Cope to send pamphlets.

Fred [inserted, in Allen's hand: MARTIN] has been collecting your various sendings to him, but I haven't seen them yet, and I doubt if we can get anything more into "ND36," as my last page count was right up to the top of the barrel. But there is always another one following on half a year later.

I didn't know that Shig had left City Lights. The place can't be the same without him.

I hope Naropa will have a great summer, and give my best to the poets. I am glad that Gregory will be there under your wing.

Very best, as ever,

James Laughlin
[in AG's hand:] Xerox for David Cope
c/o NADA Press/ B Scream
696 48th ST. S.E.
Grand Rapids, Mich 49508]

David to Allen   Feb 10, 1977

Dear Allen

3 AM. the hiss of tires spinning on snow outside my window. have been thinking about writing you about *Mind Breaths*—not that a boy like me should presume to give you a critique—what was that old Norse myth about the elder poet singing the presumptuous boy into a fen?—but only that I felt the best way to honor your book would be to pick my favorites.

I had been waiting for this book for a long time, familiar with many of the poems thru hearing them once or seeing them in small press, or on one occasion in *NY Times* mag—"Mugging," I think. Seeing them all together, plus more, is indeed a thrill. My greatest favorites are the following: "Returning to the Country for a Brief Visit"—absolute perfect clarity & simplicity; "Night Gleam"; "What I'd Like to Do," the humor here—how many times have I tried to read *Bros. Karamazov*—tho I did finish *Crime & Punishment*; "Sweet Boy, Gimme Yr Ass"—tho I'm not gay in physical sense, this is a beautiful seduction; "Manifesto"—I like you when you're cantankerous, it's one of the things I found endearing in Blake; "Sad Dust Glories," this drop of water examined in sunlight; "Ego Confession," everyone should do it—I want to be the most beloved poet of my generation; "Mugging"; "Cabin in the Rockies"; "Rolling Thunder Stones"—I like this blues, mixed, so to speak, with Am. Indian chant; "Two Dreams"—the green dwarf is great!, & rhythms in "Sludge" are excellent; "Don't Grow Old" all of it, but especially VI & VII; "Haunting Poe's Baltimore."

Now, to the "Contest of Bards"—I can say it is a poem of absolute perfection, not sure how I feel about it, stylistically. This is, if I'm not mistaken, the great long poem you wrote me about—you were on a Pan-Am jet [see note] after having spent time with a young brash boy who made you read Blake's "Jerusalem," & you were so ecstatic you summed up the basic Blakean schema for me, in your letter (which was great, I knew & understood it well, but could not have put it more succinctly myself). Now, to the poem—your style has, to me, seemed always a delicate balance between Whitman's lyricism & Blake's straight back, & it seems to me here to lack a little of the Whitman. Whether this is important, I don't know—the lines charge at me a bit, & perhaps I need to grow into them a little.

Interesting, the confrontation betw. old bard & young poet—this is a mental set played & replayed in my life time & time again—at times I've been old bard who fell asleep & had to have some crazy kid laugh in my face; & sometimes I've been that crazy kid. It goes back to your "Manifesto," awareness. Or Blake, opposition is true friendship. "The Rune"—by god, you're up in the stars—this poem should be surrounded by angels. II—I wonder, is chastity a condemnation? tho that of course is not the point here—perhaps I'm wrong, but in many ways the whole book reminds one of the 10 Oxherding Pictures, where the ox runs free & wild, crazier & crazier with desire, until the zen oxherder curbs him by force of discipline, that his life be tranquil & clear—this second section is really the climax.

The 2 final poems, "I Lay Love on My Knee," & "Love Replied," are my favorites for the sheer joy of reading them—you have attained the simplicity I first saw you searching for in "September on Jessore Road." They are bells to ring in heaven. Period.

As to the book's place in your growth—& this is really presumptuous of me, but let me speak what I feel—it's a *definite* upturn from *The Fall of America*—much more experiment, much more investigation of mental states (but then of course there's no war to contend with <at least none so close as Vietnam). I feel you have mastered what you want to do, but have yet to write your greatest poem.

Presently I'm reading *The Dharma Bums* & will begin *Book of Dreams* after that. *Dharma Bums* is a lot of fun—I remember being self-assured & pompous like that [see note]. If I ever meet Gary Snyder I'd like to go up in mountains with him—I'm not a pure wild man like him, but have spent enough time in the woods to know how to enjoy it—in fact, I bet I could show him some places around Lake Michigan that would blow his shit away. Also going to read *First Blues*, give comment if you like—I am familiar with blues thusly: Ma Rainey>Bessie Smith>Billie Holiday>Janis Joplin; early blues people Blind Blake "Police Dog Blues"; Blind Lemon Jefferson; Mississippi John Hurt, the most perfect melodious old man of them all; Son House & Robert Johnson, who had hellhounds on their trail; Memphis Minnie, who had the finest acoustic rhythm guitar of them all, also one of the first to pick up electric; Howlin' Wolf & Muddy Waters, the 2 greatest city singers, bar none; others, Leadbelly, Charlie Patton, etc., & of course the greatest blues singers of my generation The Rolling Stones, Eric Clapton, etc. I'm a Dylan fan too; tho I see him on a whole different level than these others. It seems to me this: to sing the blues one must leave one's mental set behind; or begin with the mental set & work one's way out of it, to breathe the free air. Enough! If you like, I will comment, when I've read *First Blues*. (next morning: you really oughta record them, with a good band to back you up & Dylan to sing harmony)

Have written some great new poems; a lot of compression. A sonnet for you, a la Shakespeare but free & with a youthful twist; a story of lovers in Philadelphia; & some assembly line rhapsodies out of Detroit, all of which I'll send with this letter. Hope you are doing well (what a damn fool thing to say, of course you're doing well). I'm here if you need me.

  Dave Cope

  P.S. Perhaps we should discuss the psychology of the young man & his mentor. I was reading where this relationship is necessary to every young man's development, but that often the tendency is toward alienation, where both parties feel used, in some sense. I see my rel. to you as a mentor sort of thing, & would like to be careful to make it a lasting friendship, i.e. no sour grapes. This is spelled out more clearly in sonnet for you *Love, Dave.*

David to Allen   Undated, likely May 1977

Dear Allen

  I'm sorry to write again so soon but I feel I owe you a letter—the last one lacked clarity. Strange thing my asking for a critique, wondering where I might not be clear—the next day I began reading *On the Road* again, & I kept thinking how could I ever be as clear as this? —it set off a whole chain of associations & thoughts. Thinking about my comparison of McCurry's *Machine* with Jack's work & what a flippant thought that might seem—yet seriously, Jim has energy & perception in much the same way. I understand he's sent *Delirium* to you—there's a piece of his on p. 38, & I'll send you his ms. of *Machine* this weekend. Secondly, thinking about how ambitious I might seem in my letters, & perhaps I am terribly ambitious—here I'm not sure how to deal with all my thoughts, it's a complex of feelings still too new to be clear about but I'll try to elaborate. Suddenly finding myself after all these years of working talking to you, one of the great mythical heroes of my childhood, who helped me thru so many crises of understanding, I find myself a bit confused, maybe as you must've been getting to know Dr. Williams—I sense that a little in letters in *Paterson*. Yet at the same time I know this was meant to happen, & I should attend to you as a father.

  Also, I'm not now sure if pushing my way into the spotlight would be right for me. I'd like to get to know you, & Creeley, Duncan & a few others, as good friends who could teach me what I must know, & whom I could push on the way any youth pushes his elders—there are at least 4 I know in my generation who can further & carry on what yours has done. At any rate I'm not sure making a lot of dough for publishing, or elaborate touring, or soliciting a publisher, would be right now—but rather, learning what I have to learn. A voice tells me over & over to learn patience, & I have been moving too fast.

  I guess that's all for now; I'll send McCurry's ms. with return envelope SASE. Still working on Michael McMahon's book; he's a writer full of silences & moonlight.

      Dave

Attachment: "Raleigh" poem written in May 1977, with editing notes (not, I think, in Allen's hand).

David to Allen May 1977, per superscript note in Allen's hand: "Rc'd May 77 w. True Love booklet Allen."

Dear Allen

First I want to thank you for mentioning my work to Jim Sherry of *Roof*. How were things in Boulder? It's a gorgeous day here in G. R., the grackles racing across the lawn, their funny blue heads ducking in the grass, children racing thru parking lots on sidewalks on Big Wheel trikes: I thought I should write & say where I'm at now, big ms. enclosed; & see how you're coming on your big 25 page poem of youth & age—if you're finished, & you've got a copy I'd love to see it.

Have been thru some beautiful changes last few months—got into George Harrison's last 3 records, so full of love & energy—went to church & met a beautiful priest who blesses food—even salami & beer—had lotsa visitors from across the land, Raleigh Houston LA Denver, some uptight who needed to get high & relax—

I have a suggestion, relating to correspondence: I found, with old friend Montgomery, that if we write only when full of energy, & when we have big ms. we want to share & bounce ideas off each other, we become more energized as a result, & less trapped into each others emotions & hangups. I think last winter you & I may have run too fast together for a while, & so found less to say—not that I didn't enjoy it, it was exhilarating—anyroad I thought I'd run that by you with idea of our communicating every 2-3 months or so, & keep up on where we're at.

Re reading: I went thru half my books on reading spree, feel in love with Wordsworth, I never thought of it before but he's my great uncle, & with Whitman's Civil War poems—thinking to see how he handled it, after finishing my poem "Peace." I think my present ms. is a movement beyond GO; trying to tighten up again & drive the images home in short segments, single image poems etc. Re-read your short "fly away tiny mite" postcard poem today—that is as perfect a statement as anyone's made, for my money, clear as Blake's short work, & beyond Experience.

All for now—hope you're well & happy, write soon.

Dave [in Allen's hand: (David Cope)]

PS: I also neglected to mention: I have really become involved with Gary Snyder's work, especially *The Back Country*. Could I have his address?

Allen to David Undated, likely early to mid-summer 1977
Naropa Inst. 1111 Pearl St. Boulder Colo. 80302

Dear David—

I left all three yr pamphlets with Ferlinghetti who may or may not appreciate them as I do, and who lacks money for new books, tho he is considering publishing a new City Lites Journal or a book of 3 poets I recommended. But he's unsure.

James Laughlin compiling poems for New Directions semi-annual anthology, writes (from 333 6th Ave. N.Y.C. 10014) "I wonder if I ever received the pamphlet from David Cope. The poetry books are all pretty well alphabetized, and it doesn't turn up where it should, if I had it." He's forgotten he wrote me a nice note about *Stars* a year ago—gettin' old. Anyway, please send him all <u>3</u> pamphlets anew with note I said to re-supply him. OK Allen Ginsberg

Allen to David   Ginsberg + Ferlinghetti July 11, 77

Dear David—did I send you the enclosed already? Please send them copy of your books. Also send Ferlinghetti who read my copies of all 3 books. Also can you send copies of *Go* + later book to Naropa Library (they have *Stars*) 111 Pearl St. Boulder Colo. Did *Roof* write you? Bill me for all this above. In haste
                 Love   Ginsberg
                     Allen

Missing letter David to Allen here—I had apparently asked if Ferlinghetti was tired of publishing.

Allen to David

Naropa Institute
1111 Pearl St.
Boulder, Colo. 8032
                                                                                                                           7/23/77

                         [Handwritten:] Dictated

Dear David Cope

I got both your pamphlets (i.e. mimeo and typewritten) I read both will reply more later; no Ferlinghetti is not tired of publishing; just keep him and Fred Martin at New Directions supplied with your work and each time to N.D. remind Martin that Ginsberg requested your work be shown to Laughlin. What was name of last eight by twelve booklet you sent me before *True Love* with Mae West Angel cover? [Handwritten:] I left it w/ Ferlinghetti, + he hasn't returned it yet.

David to Allen   March 27, 78

Dear Allen
       You've inspired me! Meeting you this last weekend was one of the greatest honors of my life.

Will keep in touch, especially re Naropa this summer.
                                  Dave

PS: Don't know if this poem lays too heavy a burden at your feet; I know you can do it, & hope you will. Would like to discuss the epic with you—don't see it necessarily as a monument—

particularly Wordsworth's *Prelude* or Williams' *Paterson*—feel also that preparations should be exhaustive—the rest of us should gather around you and give you strength.

David to Allen 13 April 1978

Dear Allen

Re going to Naropa—think I'll wait 'til next year—I need another year to mature, & feel I could use the money to print a limited edition of my work to date, doing it properly, which I'll do this fall.

Also, I was not properly appreciative of your blues. Forgive me— "Father Death" & "The Rune" were amazing performances.

Dave Cope

P.S. Also thanks for showing me documents on FBI late 60s.

Allen to David May 27, 78

Dear David—

Nice to meet you + family. —leaving for Naropa June 6—then a month retreat in Calif—back to N.Y. October—If you need be you can reach me in Boulder or via City Lights— Have a weird summer!—

Love
Allen

David to Allen June 6, 78

[top third of page my drawing of creator figure, hand extended downward, from Blake]

Hi!
This is fun. I hope we can continue. Also, could Robert Duncan write me & suggest a question? I'd love to bounce ideas with him too. Thanks for having faith in my work. I miss being there, maybe next year, if the money's right. Applied for grant.

Love
Dave

PS [at end of attached poem]: *Thanks*. Personal letter follows when I get time. also wrote one for Ferlinghetti / The Arab Telephone / Will send.

Attachment: "The Hydra": a lousy poem quickly abandoned.

David to Allen 1978

[postcard of The Detroit Industry Murals by Diego Rivera, at the DIA]

Dear Allen

    Back from Detroit where I read *The Tempest* & mused over this mural. Thanks again for your efforts on my behalf—I don't have it here, but was the "Rain," for Charles Reznikoff, one of the poems pub. in the 2 anthologies? Have you received *A Need for Tenderness* yet? Also, I sent you *The Clouds & Neon Eyes*, an earlier publ., to NY address. I'm waiting for City Lights to send me your latest books—read "Kral Majales" & "The Change" Friday—they still knock me out, especially "The Change" "the sun my visible father making my body visible thru my eyes!" All for now. Thanks Dave Cope

David to Allen   1978

[Anti-nuclear postcard featuring Michigan Palisades Nuclear Power Plant]

Dear Allen
I hope you got ms. mailed to City Lights; 26 pages. enclosed please find 5 sonnets to bring it up to 31—I think these are my best work to date, but haven't lived with them long enough to feel certain.

                                        love Dave

P.S. Please give me comments.

Missing letter from Allen sometime in 1978-1979: with criticisms of David's work noted in following letter.

David to Allen   in Allen's hand: postmarked Sept 25, 1979

Dear Allen
    ms. enclosed, your criticisms well-taken & thanks, for the proposed anthology. Poems roughly chronological '75-'79.
    Ferlinghetti should read David Montgomery's best work if he wants prose. Montgomery has no sense of editing—will send out brilliant & unreadable work in the same package—but he has some work more incisive than anything current in prose. Re LF's feelings about poetry—if I understand rightly: he must realize the curious socio-historical position poets my age find ourselves in. We cannot simply kick the doors down & announce ourselves, changing the way people think & relate; the doors are gone, the path has been amply marked & well-trodden before us. No, I think our position is more a matter of quietly & as simply as possible recording the great & small events of our times. Our century's been fortunate in having so many brilliant & earth-shaking writings—perhaps our (mine & Andy's & Antler's, as well as the Iowa Actualists & Robert Borden's & al) task is simply to learn to record without obsession. Also—what else has Robert Borden written? His Vietnam pieces in *CL* #4 are *incredible!*

Any other underground political/spiritual news I should know? Thanks for getting Eric Lerner to send me *Zero*; besides Roshi's essay, your frog in the old pond is a fine humorous poem—also G.S.'s Willys pickup poem (I've spent half the summer hauling horseshit & pine needles myself).

Re ms. if you suggest any changes call me collect (616) 531-1442. Also my zip is 49418.

Great hearing from you! & I hope these poems sit well. Send me mags with your new works.

Dave

PS: If you're travelling betw. Chicago & Ann Arbor-Detroit, stop here for the night. Double bed, walnut trees & good veg meal!

Allen Ginsberg, The Lion for Real sessions, 1984.
Photo by Christopher Funkhouser.

Allen, Peter Hale, Chris Ide, David just off camera. Naropa 4th of July, 1980s
Photo by Steve Miles.

Tom Swartz, David Cope, Cassidy Clausen, Mark Christal atop Mt. Audubon, 1982. Photo by Mark Christal.

1980-1989: Building a Poetry Life

Carl Rakosi and David Cope on Allen's Marine Street balcony, summer Objectivist Conference at Naropa, 1987. Photo by Allen Ginsberg.

David to Allen Jan 17, 1980

Dear Allen

Well first of all *Thanks* for *Poems All Over the Place*. Struck by the line:

> "my handwork remains when prisons fall because the hand is compassion"

Want to hear you read "These States to Miami Convention"—I heard it in my imagination—"ahs" extended into long soft breaths. Pleased to see "Junk Mail" which you read when I saw you in D.C.— my friend Gary's wife Lin (who doesn't read much & was somewhat reluctant to come to the reading!) ecstatically later talked how you'd transformed the most ordinary things to make for higher understanding. Suzy got a charge out of "For Creeley's Ear." *T.S. Eliot*—strange to associate him with CIA types, when his ear was so perfect—but then Pound had strange connections too. The real asskicker for me tho was *from Journals*, the question of how heavily we were manipulated—wish the whole notebook you had could be put in print. In the end, I wonder—in my own situation, at that time, I'd probably have gone crazy LSD or bricked windows regardless of FBI + CIA—I had horrible frustrations trapped in U of M academia headed (it seemed) only towards a corporate teaching job; all my friends (e.g. Gary Schmidt, tender hearted roommate) selling their dreams down the river for IBM-type jobs, & sick with themselves for doing it, other friends butchered in Vietnam, & first LBJ talking a shitline then Nixon whose very face provoked me to rage—coupled with then unresolved hatred for my father who all this time was quoting Sumner & talking about the domino theory—

  Well, you set off a string of firecrackers in this quarter! Anyroad, to other news (first, *thanks again*) I've finished big ms. 135 pages plus small 48 page ms for Ferlinghetti enclosed for your inspection—then I guess mail it back to me w. suggestions, I'll consider them & send on to City Lights. Jim C. "forewarned" me to seek best deal & retain rights; as I have no experience on this level, I wonder what would be a fair deal?

  Thanks also for your intro page. I'll do 10 more complete mss. (135 pages) & begin sending them out, 1 publisher at a time, also to translators. Is the Lebel you mention the same Lebel in the Fugs song about "Early Verlaine Bread Crust Fragments"? What is Tuli Kupferberg doing now? Strange to send poems to mags you've recommended—I always felt they were a bit above me, like *Poetry*—always aimed at mags for unknowns & felt most of these must've been for Robert Lowell types (not to knock Lowell, I have & admire some of his work)

  Man, am I excited about coming to Boulder! (strange situation, trying to work out weird feelings about our miscarriage, comforting Suzy who's naturally exhausted (almost like giving birth, yet no birth to show) & depressed; at the same time getting crazy reading *Visions of the Daughters of Albion* aloud to myself, or rummaging thru Chaucer with idea of teaching students there natural melodic rhythm via their voicing poems aloud. Anyways I'm excited by these prospects & by seeing you again. Send me Andy's stuff. I'll keep plugging away here.

           Love
           Dave

P.S. 135 pg. ms follows in a few days.

Allen to David   Naropa 1111 Pearl Street Boulder Colo. 80302 A. Ginsberg Feb. 18, 1980

Dear David: To clarify matters a little—since I working remote-control so to speak, thru Jim Cohn who's been industrious—What I'm trying to do is 1.) Assemble all your work I dig most as gems, solid hard 2.) Cut and edit + retype for your consideration a few major or minor poems which seem otherwise flawed but could be reduced to hard elements. All this as a first stage to preparing a giant (so it seems) ms. from which to choose 48 pps. from the City Lights Books of 3 poets 48 pps. each. It looks like you have a lot more material than that. I've done first editing, Jim C. does retyping + advice. Antler's withdrawn his mss. but it can't fit on page properly, + Ferlinghetti does not want to go beyond what he, somewhat doubtfully offered—a book of 3 poets. I've asked Robert Meyers if he has a mss. Your own book looks so big + good maybe we should try out Black Sparrow or N.Y. for a big whole book? I don't know. I want to do good but am overwhelmed with high blood pressure this year from being too ambitious in plans + dreams + frustrated in working them out— Quiet Words [sic] fine.

right sidebar: P.S. Feb. 19 I've gone thru half the mss. now, zeroing in on poems or workable parts to think best with work we've done already—OK Allen. I have to digest + integrate yr letter.

Attachment: Allen's recommendation letter to publishers:

Naropa Institute
1111 Pearl Street
Boulder Colorado
80302—March 1, 1980

To Whom it May Concern:

    I have been much absorbed in David Cope's poetry as necessary continuation of tradition of lucid grounded sane objectivism in poetry following the visually solid practice of Charles Reznikoff & William Carlos Williams. Though the notions of "objectivism" were common for many decades among U.S. poets, there is not a great body of direct-sighted "close to the nose" examples of poems that hit a certain ideal objectivist mark— "No ideas but in things" consisting of "minute particulars" in which the "natural object is always the adequate symbol", works of language wherein "the mind is clamped down on objects" and where these "Things are symbols of themselves." The poets I named above specialized in this refined experiment, and Pound touched on the subject as did Zukofsky and Bunting, and lesser but interesting figures such as Marsden Hartley in his little known poetry, and more romantic writers such as D.H. Lawrence. In this area of phanapoeiac "focus," the sketching of particulars by which a motif is recognizably significant, David Cope has made, by the beginning of his third decade, the largest body of such work that I know of among poets of his own generation.

    I have corresponded with him for years and in the last half year have helped edit a selection which City Lights plans to anthologize in a book of three poets (Cope, Andy Clausen & Robert Meyers—each young, unpublished and touched with some original genius in my opinion.) After eliminating dross, there remains a book of 130 pages, of which City Lights can publish only a 40 page selection. I suggested to David Cope that he send his work out more widely for publication, and offered to write a short introductory note for that purpose, which this page serves.

Sincerely yours,
Allen Ginsberg

Allen to David, notes on changes.   Undated.

[Notes in another's hand re editing David's manuscript, with Allen's notes at bottom. This sheet is really a crib sheet for the revisions Allen sent me—though I no longer have copy of that letter.]

[In another's hand (green ink)]:

Allen.

Collected Poems David Cope

        Typos.   Black Book (line drawn around Black Book)

1. "music" line 4 change "a" > "at"
2. "Watching TV During A Snowstorm": p. 40
    Change "befor eme" > "before me"
3. "The Art Museum" p. 82
    Changing "building" > "builder"

—Revisions marked in Table of Contents w "X"
    & noted in xerox text by "Revised"
—As is poems marked in T of C w/ "check mark"
    & noted in xerox by "save"

[In Allen's hand (black ink)]:

    This is collection of my choices of Cope's entire work, with suggested revisions. Sent to him for City Lights selection, for him to check out. Done Winter-Spring 1980.

Dave to Allen   c. July 1980

Poems:

Thank you! Thank you!

jagged nut-brown upthrust
rock thru which lightning arcs!
wide valley, spruce & pine
    roots thrust into rock,
chipped & chiseled stones,

little glades of
white round flowers, rockhillside
yellow & orange white lavender,
seeds in the air,
racing white water, aspen groves
& thunder! thunder everywhere!

Flowering wild
columbine, lavender surrounds
white lotus center.

Text surrounding poems:

By God, you're the greatest! I stand before you in awe! love David Cope

PS: There is a God in Heaven who watches our every deed & knows what we do. Love Daisy He he he it's truth! Your own father & mother are watching you! & Dante & Blake, Wordsworth, Shelley Sidney & Spenser & Shakespeare & Marlowe & Sappho Homer Catullus Aristophanes the whole perfect singing crowd who know & love you now.

David to Allen likely fall 1980

Dear Allen

Is it possible somebody there could xerox a copy of Marsden Hartley's poems for me? I wrote Brandon Press (Boston), the last publisher of his works—no copies left & none contemplated. I'd pay for a xerox copy.

Second, do you know 2 or 3 good rare book stores I could write to, to get a copy like yours?

These poems are still singing in my head daily.

Man, I dig having all the friends I made out there! I get news every few days from Boulder—almost everybody had at least one poem that struck me—the task is getting them all to send me these poems for a Boulder *Big Scream*. Received <u>excellent</u> work from Tom Swartz.

Read most of Andy's work. I have definite favorites, tho I'm pretty sure somebody else should help him edit—someone whose style is closer to his.

All for now. Hello to Peter.

Love
Dave

PS: Read Sappho, Mary Barnard's translation. Ah!

David to Allen 1980 Oct. 20

Dear Allen

First of all <u>Thanks</u> for Marsden Hartley book; I've read & re-read the poems & never tire of them. Check enclosed to help defray the cost of xeroxing them; if Naropa paid, perhaps they could use it toward their building fund. Thanks also for manuscript of John Carl's poems.

  I feel I should apologize for not writing sooner—have been busy as hell working & preparing house & garden for winter. Finished Jim Cohn's book, but no word from him as yet. I am going to publish *Big Scream Goes West* next, & then a chapbook of my new short works. 2 poems writ in Boulder published on *Dial-a-Poem* today (Oct. 8), *Zero* has some they haven't decided on yet.

  A new serenade for you enclosed & a few others.

  Have been reading Roman history lately—Suetonius + Tacitus. When the prose gets to me I've been poring thru *Mind Breaths*, reading here & there. So many remarkable works in there.
      All—aha—all for now.

      Love
      Crazy Dave

[goofball drawing of myself with grass stem protruding from mouth]

Attached: "October Serenade" [note: this & 3 others after hearing recordings of Robert Lowell reading his *Life Studies*], "Thanksgiving," and "Abandoned Hotel," handwritten mss.

David to Allen Dec. 1980

Dear Allen
Where to go? Neither here nor there. Not this, not that.

  "PEACE, PEACE, HE IS NOT DEAD"

  the rarest flower in the field!
  crushed!

  40 years, a short life.
  yet he came full circle,
  beginning & ending with purpose
   & enthusiasm,
  surrounding pain with love.

  mourn the songs he can't give us
   in old age,
  the sorrow of an innocent child,
  sorrow that someday'll abate—
  mourn for the murderer,

    whose pistol smokes, defeated—
    but don't mourn one
    who could give his heart away.

    clear air, new dawn.
    the wheel turns again.
    what new soul comes down,
        as clear as he,
    to sing our hearts into love?

[Right sidebar across from poem:] continue the work learning & teaching kindliness, courtesy, honesty & clarity; planting; sharing thoughts & kindnesses; looking to those who've been forgotten; stating with clarity sources of the problems; compassion even for sick politicians; attempt to listen more attentively. Too big a list? No. It should be done, within human limits. I cannot hope, but hope to cope.

[Below poem:] hoo-hah! Forgive the length of this letter, I've had 1000 ecstasies & visions since we last talked (maybe one or two not completely nuts!) Letter from Ferlinghetti who's puzzled with "objectivist" poems— "cameras can do that!" but he wants me to visit someday. I wrote back saying I'm not objectivist per se but wrote what moved me, handling experience with coolness & clarity, not "leading" the reader. (My father said greatest handicap of American workers was western savior complex & leader-follower anxieties not living & functioning in a circle—he's trying to apply Japanese labor relations concepts to his business, but I found these thoughts instructive re role of poet—no leader or guru, but only 1 in a circle of many—not directing thoughts of others, but positing actual experiences as shared thoughts.) I like L.F.'s reticence however! He makes me work for friendship!

Al Pearlman got me a reading underground coffee house in Ann Arbor. I consciously adopted Corso's swivel-hips reading style, & Al got me a little drunk—gave much looser performance (& had fun) than in Boulder where I was still a scared kid reading for idols. Also learning to work the microphone—still hate the fucking things tho. You woulda died laughing, crazy dada-rock act that followed me on; androgynous kid in black underwear & combat boots wandering thru the band humping the air. Also met Ken Mikolowski, finally. Learned my old teacher Robert Hayden is dead—his health was always bad. A tender man with a tender touch; he could never figure your writings out, read us "Kral Majales" once & wanted us to talk it out, which we did, & fairly well, too. Tight with words, short & to the point.

Strange mail—<u>BITTER ANGRY</u> young poets—5 or 6 in the last month screaming in my ear. Write 'em back & get more screams back [sidebar continuation of sentence, w. arrow >] unclear screams—unfocused—shouted abstractions or anger at 60s radicals for "inability to accept the modern world" (?!)—anger for no publication, tho poems don't warrant it—yet. I worry that nat'l poet-scene is too fragmented again—perhaps yearly Sioux-style gathering of tribes is in order, knit up the broken connections & start helping each other & all these young crazies along. Utopian dream?

Working on *BIG SCREAM* GOES WEST, all Boulder poets Swartz Ruggia Clausen (Ramona) Sgambati Pearlman Pirofsky Wojczuk Ross Banta etc. Have revised *Shorter Selected Poems 74-80* into 52 pages all shorts including newer poems I sent you in late Oct. + short poems that worked well in public readings. Nothing longer. Swartz & Wojczuk have a mag out—haven't got it yet.

Hello Peter!

Met a grey panther thru my anti-nuke teach-ins (concentrating more now on weapons proliferation, MX, defense spending & implications. What we gonna do with Haig in there!) who sent me to an old folks home where I read Hartley & Frost to shut-ins.

Planted balsam fir, 2 mugho pines, 4 junipers before winter came on (also 2 spruce, 2 white pines, peach, 2 arbor vitae & 2 dogwoods, 1 magnolia earlier this year). burning bush, mock orange, rhododendron, bittersweet, honeysuckle. If you're coming thru Chicago A2 or Detroit, lemme know. I'll try to make it.

Love Dave

P.S. L. F., just read; thinking of Lennon "such men as these do rise above our worst imaginings." Yas suh! [drawing of myself in shades with grass stem hayseeds protruding from mouth]

Allen to David   Frankfurt December 14 [or 17] 1980

Dear David:
      Peter + I + young guitarist been travelling in Europe the last 2 months—Jugoslavia + Hungary, Austria Germany Switzerland Amsterdam + doubling back down the Rhine before flying home tomorrow. Here's Mad King Ludwig's Bavarian New Swan castle. Communist Bureaucrats a drag, Capitalist violent exploitation a drag, Innocent Anarchism lacks protection (like also John Lennon.) Where to go? —Hope —you're well. Ferlinghetti said before I left he was doubtful he'd have the money to do our book. What did you think of my choices? I'll be in N.Y. till March except for readings/travel.
As ever, Allen Ginsberg.

Allen to David   [Stamped from NYC, on Lamar Hotel Stationary, Houston]   Dec. 30, 1980

Dear David—
      Back from Hungary + Europe—Houston. Red Bureaucracy a drag, got yr letter, "Don't mourn one who could give his heart away" is OK on Lennon.
      Too much paper I'm fatigued, can't write better. Just to say Happy New Year this scribble.
      "Bitter Angry" young poets, I get lotsa that electric, over decades. Lennon took a bit himself.

  I got the *New Blood* mag— "The Landlady" + "Abandoned Hotel" perfect. "Lelia" I liked, but couldn't figure exactly what "the news" was, she kicked the bucket? "Thanksgiving" less sharp, tho a unified theme.
  No heart for letters.

Regards to Ken Mikolowski.

Allen

When I get some strength I'll try to work on publisher for yr book again. Try Fred Martin New Directions?

Allen to David   Jan 1981

Dear David—
  Back from months in Europe. I liked *Fresh Blood*, "Landlady" & "Abandoned Hotel," & also "Lelia," though in the latter, but there's something missing (some clue)—she died? Not sure? Of what? I don't know—something left out?
  Up late (1:40 AM) answering piles of mail. Antler's book's out. Ferlinghetti fudged on the book with you + Clausen + Meyers. How's he responding to your charms now?
  Have you tried Black Sparrow, and Blue Wind Press? And Jeffrey Miller of Cadmus Ed. Box 4725 Santa Barbara, Calif. 93130?
  Happy New Year. I'm exhausted for the moment. Regards to Suzie.
As ever
Allen
Keep it up!

A Quiet Life—Thanks, plenty nice poems there. For Politics— "American Protest" is the sharpest.

David to Allen   c. Jan 81

Dear Allen
  Hey man check the other side of this page! Got your card—am writing you from a mop closet at work, among piles of toilet paper, trashbags, singlefold towels, electrical panels & parking lot light boxes, my friend maniacally playing piano & shouting "I'm OK! I'm OK!" on portable tape player. This is my office (ha!)
  Tom Swartz & Charlie Ross cruising here at end of this coming week—Ross's getting married to his Mary Lu, they'll pick up a car, a wedding present, & visit us, where I've prepared a crazy drunken poem reception for 'em! *Big Scream* out (basically, same folks as in *New Blood*). Lotsa calls & mail. Ruggia in NYC tending bar at Rockefeller Center, lives somewhere near you, on Park Avenue South (303?), his love new born! I'm so happy! Will send you *Big Scream* when I do next mailing—a week or two, no money.
  Saw your beautiful poem "Did someone steal Mona Lisa's smile" in *Rolling Stone*. We cried.

As to big time publication—Ferlinghetti said he had no money for the 3 man book project. The publishing scene is undoubtedly as depressed now as the rest of the economy, & I felt he was correct in assessing possibilities of a new book getting somewhere; further, poets my age still need to do our own homework, "establishing names" in many cities etc. I think it's important to gather in the friendships I made last summer—we are all learning from each other & building energy at an incredible rate now, & that's where I see importance. The big printing may or may not come later—it doesn't worry me too much, as I'm having a ball now. I will try one of these publishers perhaps this spring (tho I think with time, patience & familiarity, I could get in with City Lights, which is where I really want to be. I need to go to San Francisco & meet that scene yet—maybe in a year or two.

Lelia poem—she died. That wasn't the point, however—hopefully the last line has enough of an air of finality—hell, the news is always bad—the point being she wouldn't listen & observe the signs—her sickness, her husband's concern—& her body made her pay for it. There's a companion poem to this, "Evening Service," which Tom didn't publish. She was a fine old black lady, in any case—suspicious as hell of whites, but ready & willing to lend her last dollar to anyone who said he needed it—

Now reading Everson's *Residual Years*—a birthday present from Suzie—his grape ploughing & picking poems really appeal to me, as well as *some* of the less imagistic/objectivist pieces—his address to Churchill, advocating a higher morality (hate that word, morality, tho he uses it as well as one might). Ferlinghetti send me his *Landscapes*, which I love (tho "The Love Nut" is a rather peculiar poem) especially the famous poems "Adieu à Charlot"— which *woke* me 2 years ago—the most a poem could expect of its reader!, & the Moscone/Milk elegy.

Well, all for now. I'm 33—1/3 of the way to 100! —& just building up a head of steam! Hope you're well—talk to Al Pearlman about an Ann Arbor reading next Fall—335 E. Ann, Ann Arbor Mi 48104—maybe forward—he's becoming a real impresario of poem readings. No ink—shit! E-hah!

E-hah! Love Dave

[hand-scrawled poster advertising reading on back of first page:]

Flash in the Pan Readings

Presents

AN EVENING OF POETRY & MADNESS

UNHEARD OF ECSTASIES

—bring poems & guitars, open reading
Featured poets

TOM SWARTZ, poet & madman, editor at *New Blood*

CHARLIE ROSS, angel of shifting gears, former editor at Bombay Gin, head honcho Boulder Poetry Project

DAVID MONTGOMERY, the infamous M, guitar maniac,
poet & novelist, film maker, editor of Lemming Press

—the place: Dave Cope's house
2782 Dixie SW
LITTLE GOLD HOUSE

We start at 8:00 Saturday night JANUARY 24

Allen to David   Jan 16, 1981

Dear David—
    Why don't you enter this? Send me a xerox a choice of a dozen poems packaged up and I'll send them on to Grace Schulman whom I've seen recently.
    Otherwise it's a sorta dreary poesy center.
                  As ever
                    Allen
I think *Nation* might like some of the boat people Vietnam poems. or whatever—
    Did you apply for NEA grant—? Deadline Feb 15. Do it!

David to Allen   in Allen's hand: rec'd 20 Jan 81

Dear Allen

    Here's entire Vietnamese Sequence to date as per your request, to be sent to Grace Schulman for *The Nation* contest. Thanks for your help!
    I bet that March 23 reading Kinnell & Levertov would be great. I saw Levertov read once, & was impressed with her quiet style. Never saw Kinnell—tho Suzy has, & enjoyed it immensely—I have 2 of his books, some poems that grab me—

                  Love

                      Dave [in Allen's hand: Cope]

David to Allen 1981 April 4

Dear Allen

    Here's some colored eggs in a silver bowl just for you. Sent my "Selected Poems '74-81" to University of Pittsburg poetry competition (1st prize publication + $1000), & also to Tom Lanigan at Humana Press who apparently heard of me thru you. Maybe I'll finally get the damn thing out & be freed to go on to other things. Shortened it to 87 pages—cut out about 60 pages & replaced some with short housecleaning + ghetto poems from last year—more accessible now. Also I used "Introductory Note" you wrote me last March as a preface. Should the book be published, may I use that 1st paragraph (detailing objectivists + ideas on theory etc, my connection to it) for an Introduction? (Second paragraph unnecessary, as it mostly deals with Ferlinghetti's now nixed 3 man anthology).

    Just got Len Roberts' *Cohoes Theater* which you'd recommended also. I published him in *Big Scream* in '77 I think—he doesn't recall—amazing how these people come back into my life. Good book. He needs to visit Naropa.

    Well all for now. Charlie and Mary Lu came home to bury her mother. The hard truth, but much learning. Garden's in, I'm busy with my yard every day.

Dave

Attachment: complete letter from Allen recommending my work, with my sidebar note on first paragraph: "Would like this for intro OK?"

David to Allen 1981 Dec. 1

Dear Allen

    Two questions: do you have an address for Humana Press, somewhere in New Jersey? I sent complete manuscript of my poems 74-80 to the editor there last May. He promised to give me word on it by July but as yet have heard nothing. In the interim, I lost his address.

    Second, could I have George Oppen's address. Have written a poem about poets—stories about or told by—in which Mary Oppen recounted for us a story about autumn or midsummer bonfires the French (Provençal?) people dance to—she & George walked with us out to midsummer eve bonfire at GVSC in '72 [see note: 1973]. This was during Nat'l Poetry Festival where you sat & talked with Oppen & Reznikoff & Duncan & Rexroth—I was a young student bedazzled. I wanted to write the Oppens to get the story straight for the poem.

    If you're too busy I of course understand

    Your reading in Detroit best I've seen in years.

    Magazine article enclosed—*West Michigan* mag wanted "experts" in various fields to choose their favorites—I thought you'd enjoy it.

    Reading Pound again. Incredible renunciation at end of *Personae*. Why I never got it before I dunno.

    All for now love Dave

PS: Please tell Peter I continue to read + enjoy his *Clean Asshole Poems*, that book one to go back to again + again, the sweetest nature I've known. D.

Allen to David Jan 7, 82 7 AM

Dear David

        Thos Lanigan
        Humana Press Inc
        Crescent Manor
        POB 2148 Clifton, N.J.
        201-773-4389

    Up all night answering letters, aching back. Been working a little with Clash, a british rock group, improving lyrics + singing basso, one cut.
        Plutonian Ode's out, Poems 1977-80.
        I don't have Oppen's #—
        Geo Oppen
        2811 Polk St. S. F. Cal. 9419
        415-771-1615

    I love your poetry as ever. Sorry the (your) name got fucked up in *Time* or was it *People* mag. I ws trying + tried again in present *Amer. Book Review* to refer publishers to your poems C + you.)

    Going to Nicaragua for 1 week, late January. Travelling a lot. Clausen is on Committee on Poetry Farm, RD 2 Cherry Valley, N.Y. Keep sending me your mimeo pamphlets, I read them the day I get them + am always pleased in fact moved delighted knocked out when you hit a solid ball clear visible out of the park into the what was it trees or darkness outside?

    Have you sent poems ever to Robt Creeley
        Eng Dept
        SUNY AB
        Buffalo, N.Y.?
    Peter'll appreciate yr word, encouragement.
        Allen
    Regards to family + Happy New Year

Attachment: Dec. 9, 1981 *Time Magazine* letter from Allen to editor:

Allen Ginsberg
P.O. Box 582
Stuyvesant Station
New York, New York 10009

Time
Time & Life Building

Rockefeller Center
New York, New York, 10020

December 9, 1981

Dear Sirs,

    I was happy to mention several unpublished young poets for your readers' notice in your reportage of my reading of "Howl" (and new poems and songs) at McMillin Theatre (Dec. 7, '81). I'm glad to see you name-dropped at least one: David Cope, 2782 Dixie SW., Grandville, Michigan, 49418, editor of *"Big Scream"*/ Nada Press. However, you referred to him as "David Pope in Grand Rapids." Some brilliant avant-garde publisher among your readers may find this correction useful and seek out Mr. Cope. He or she might also print the powerful unpublished poems of Andy Clausen, R.D. 2, Cherry Valley, N.Y. 13320.

        Sincerely,
        Allen Ginsberg

You have permission to print this letter without changes. If any changes are useful, please consult me in advance.

C.C. William A Henry III
    David Cope

David to Allen

1982 Jan. 9

Dear Allen

Got your letter, & sent booklets to Oppen + Creeley. Read all of Oppen's works that I have yesterday. That man is a *deep* well. I hope to meet him again sometime—would probably be awed speechless.

Cold here today— -8 degrees, clear, sunny.

    Lanigan at Humana Press wants to publish my book, but (1) has other commitments (scientific writings) he has to fulfill first, and (2) is afraid of taking a big loss—he published one other poetry book, which sold only 200 copies. He is considering contacting Book People per distribution, but I wonder if there are things I could do to help persuade him. I'm headed to Maryland this summer, wonder if (how) I could set up reading tour, possibly hit Wash. D. C., New Jersey & New York (wanted to take train up to N.J. to see Ruggia + Rixon anyways.).

    Your mention of mine & Andy's work in various publications is a real heartening boost for me. The time is coming. I never hear from Andy, would like one of his long chants for *Big Scream*, but . . .

    Have a radio show with David Montgomery singing his songs between my readings, to be aired in February on WFMU 91.1 Fridays at 5:30, in New Jersey. If you're in NYC sometime then you might catch it. We had a lot of fun doing it.

    Ferlinghetti sent me *Plutonian Ode* review copy, arrived 2 days before Christmas. No lengthy review here, but let us say I read it 4 times straight thru, knocked out. Am purchasing 3 other copies for friends. Great to hear you are working with Clash—they've been a personal fave of mine for 2 years now, & I always felt, seeing your readings, that you needed a band of that caliber to back you on rock & blues poems. (Also like it when you + Peter do Australian song sticks numbers—lotta great rhythm there.) Been listening to Dylan Thomas recorded works—his vocal modulations are amazing!

Time magazine interview brought reporters from local media on the run, wanting to know if I planned to lead revolutions + get 6 year olds to try dope. Their image of you is at best humorous—I tried to explain Pound's Don'ts + Dos, Reznikoff's objectivism, cut-ups & "cinematic technique," but got the definite impression they weren't interested in intelligence. O well, on to better things!

Hope you're doing great!

> Love,
> Crazy Dave

[Ms. brief poem, "The Box of Fish," later abandoned, follows letter on same sheet.]

David to Allen   1982 May 28

Dear Allen

Received yet another flyer on the Kerouac Conference today, requesting info as to whether I'm coming. I appreciated your earlier invitation via Jane Faigo, but am afraid I don't know whether I'll be able to make it yet. Swartz has offer to let me stay at his place in tent in the backyard (I don't have money for dorm rooms, hotel rooms, etc.) & I may—or may not—be able to borrow money for travel expenses. I understand your need to have dollars to work with; I've had my paychecks cut $140 a month, & it hurts. I'll let you know whether I'm coming as soon as it becomes clear to me.

As to the conference itself—are we simply reliving old dreams? Still driving that stolen car that gets 10 miles a gallon—at best? Man, I hope not. The idea of meeting Ferlinghetti, Creeley, Burroughs, Snyder, turns me on—that's why I'll come if I can. I love some of Kerouac's work—his wonderful jazz line & exuberance—tho at times he degenerates into the saddest kind of self-pity. I've seen friends of mine go down the tubes like that, too, so it's not something I can't understand, or am taking at second or third hand . . . I look for something new, something different from what came before.

On another level, I think, a farewell party, a last gasp before we're all blown to hell, Buddhists & poets & sensitive plants—burned into bits of dust, shall these bones live?

Ah shit, I'm probably going on too long. What the fuck you been doing, busy as hell? We gonna stop the world, or what?

OK, here's my news. Book to be published by Humana Press, probably out in January—I trimmed ms. you & [Jim] Cohn helped me with to 60 pages (cut out another 35) then added 24 pages new work. If you don't mind the bragging, this is going to be one heavy first book—no crap whatsoever.

Lotsa publication for new poems. Didja see that *GR Press* article they did on me? Insert telephone conversation with you, damn nice things you said.

I've got a thousand questions on promotion—I want this book to sell, & I'll work as hard at it as you do, but need some guidelines. You got any time for that, or know somebody who does? I'm geared, I just need to take off. We got another poetry renaissance coming, maybe a last flowering—the energy's there, it's just got to have something to grab onto and fly with! Antler, Clausen, Ruggia, chomping at the bit. & many more.

Ha! Enough bullshit: it's in our hands.

Write me, or call, you crazy old fucker. Remember that poetry kid in Baltimore who made you read Blake all night & yelled at you to stop being a "poetry businessman"?

Love
Crazy Dave Cope

PS: Hello to Peter, his book still a favorite. I lend out now & then, but quick snatch it back.

David to Allen 1982 Jun. 21

Dear Allen

Finances straightened out, so I'll be out to Kerouac Festival, with luck. I've got a lot to learn; will be attentive. Thanks for invite.

Dave Cope

[On same sheet, manuscript of "Rexroth Gone," an important early poem later published in *Quiet Lives*, my first book, in March of 1983.]

David to Allen after July 2 (last date of Kerouac Festival), before Nov. 1982

Dear Allen

Here's new *Big Scream* I hope you'll enjoy it. Am really pleased to have Andy & Antler under same cover. Busy: besides this issue, just did local "artists against nuclear war" reading & got on TV news for performance; 2 more readings in the next 2 weeks, & am helping some younger poets set up their poetry collective, "Twilight Tribe."

Well, did you survive the conference? Lot of energy there, must've been tiring. I enjoyed meeting Ferlinghetti, & appreciated opportunity to read with Peter & Jack Micheline. If you're ever doing poetry reading tour of Midwest, would you consider reading with me, say, in 5 cities? (I could take a week off from work, "sabbatical," if I gave them enough notice—say, a month in advance.) If I could get $100 a reading + travel expenses, it could be profitable for me, & more importantly, we could get a chance to just sit & talk & read some poems back & forth as I did with Cohn & Ruggia & Swartz at Kerouac Festival—really get into things & get to know each other—seems like every time we've met, too many demands on you to relax & move beyond the surface. Well anyways, just a suggestion!

Other—have read a lot of Shelley & Browning since I got home, & am tutoring myself in Old English. Will be taking a class in German this fall—Tom Jepsen got me all excited about expressionists, so I'm following up there . . .

Saw the Clash here in town—had opportunity to meet them & talk after the show, but I was tired & I assume they were, so maybe another time . . .

All for now. Hello to Peter!

Love

Dave Cope

PS really getting off on rhythmic structures in O. Eng. Poems—great on the tongue
    [followed by first 3 lines of "Eard Stapa," The Wanderer]

Allen to David   November 7, 1982

Dear David:
        Enclosed typed note useful re readings.
        Randy Roark at Poetics dept. will contact you for a bloc of poetry for a little scream we're editing here. I'll leave Dec. 3 for NY> Paris etc. Scandinavia.

in haste as usual
Allen Ginsberg

Allen to David   November 1982
Boulder, Co.

Dear David,
        I would like to give readings with you but have no date in the Midwest now, only the East and South. Will be free some weeks in March-April 1983 if you can set up any readings with me near your territory. I'll be glad to give you one third of my fee, as my fee is under $2000—that's a bit of money.
        However, itinerary and fees have to be arranged with my agent Charles Rothschild (3330 E. 48 St., New York City, 10017, 212-752-8753). He can also supply precis biography and photos a la professional agent. I'll send him a note. Secretary <u>Maxine</u> will handle.

        This is in haste—off to Europe Dec. 3 from N.Y. till February. This note gives you the o.k. to arrange readings for us—

Love Allen

David to Allen   1982 Nov. 16

Dear Allen
        Thanks for your response on reading idea! I'll check into a March/April Milwaukee-Chicago-G.R.-Ann Arbor-Detroit tour then; Antler'll be in Milwaukee then—perhaps I could split my share with him & do a triple bill. Also my book of selected poems from Humana due out then too—a good promotion for that. I can do the driving.
        Will call Rothschild within the week & discover your exact dates so I can pursue itinerary + other data he can give of help.
        Have a great trip, & hope to see you next Spring.

Love

                              Dave
Sidebar with line around it: Hello to Peter. 4 dumptruck loads of leaf mulch of [for] my garden this Fall.

PS. Reading Williams again now—
                    ". . . difficult
         to get the news from poems
                yet men die miserably every day
                    for lack
         of what is found there . . ."
PPS. Also working on a BIG anthology of my generation's poems/poets which I'll try to market via list you sent me years ago. I'm excited!

Allen to David   Charleville, Dec 21, 82

Dear David—Finally came to Poetic Holyland, Rimbaud's home town—staying 2 nites in his old apartment—listening to incomprehensible French lectures on Rimbaud + alchemy. How sad his dark old wooden steep stairway, + the toilet in his old flat! —Love Allen G.

David to Allen   between Dec 21, 1982 and March 12, 1983.

Dear Allen
I neglected to ask your permission to use the statement you made about my work & its relation to Williams, Reznikoff et al, as a foreword to *Quiet Lives*. Am sorry about this—it's a dumb oversight on my part, & I hope you'll forgive me. The book'll probably be printed by the time you get back from Europe; if you have problems with my using the statement, please call me collect at 616 531 1442, & perhaps we can work something out (am not sure what financial arrangements, etc., are entailed in printing a foreword to a book; am ready to work with whatever goes—). Beyond this, I've worked on proof pages for the book tonight, & your statement makes a fine foreword to my book (we deleted the last paragraph, which details Ferlinghetti's aborted plan for a book of 3 poets—me, Clausen & Meyers, keeping only that portion that *Ferro Botanica* published as an introduction to a selection of my poems in its second issue).

Other—I'll be in NYC March 11-16 for the Shindar reading with me, Andy & Antler, and for a reading & two workshops with elementary kids in Hoboken. Will be staying with Ruggia (813 Willow, Hoboken 07030—201 798 0781), & will get ahold of you then.

Your postcard from Charleville warmed my whole day. Rimbaud was an early discovery for me—senior year in high school, I think. Last year, I learned Villon's work for the first time, amazed at the correspondences in outlook, the sweet-sour taste of the lines, that also flavor Rimbaud's & Baudelaire's work, for me.

Presently reading Twain's *Life on the Mississippi*—what a character.

Please excuse typing—I've been doing business all day, & it seemed I oughta get everything in here quickly. Hope you had a great trip, & welcome back to the land of quiet breaths in the middle of neon!

Love
Dave

David to Allen   1983 May 14

Dear Allen

     Do you have Follett publ. company's address, & perhaps an editor I could contact there? I've completed an anthology of 14 poets my age, including Antler, Robert Borden, Janet Cannon, Andy, Jim Cohn, myself, Elizabeth Kerlikowske, Jeff Poniewaz, Bob Rixon, Ron Rodriguez, Jim Ruggia, Al Sgambati, Tom Swartz & Nina Zivancevic, & thought Follett might be a good company to send it to, because of their young Am. poets book Paul Carroll edited years ago. The book's about 160 pages, with photos, biographies, + acknowledgements complete—it's a pretty tight anthology.

     Also, do you have Amiri Baraka's address?—and would he be receptive to helping me locate younger black poets? Other. Didja get the *Quiet Lives* book? I asked Lanigan to send you another paperback. Book is selling well here in GR with little publicity so far, & Humana Press has sent out copies to 22 major review outlets.

I have *thoroughly* enjoyed your records.

Am now writing short essays on Sp. Poets for local bi-lingual newspaper: 1 on Machado, 1 on Guillen & Martí, 1 on "my favorite Renaissance Sp. Poems" (incl. anonymous villancicos, short lyrics of Lope de Vega, one of Gongora's burlesques & "Llama de Amor Viva" by San Juan de la Cruz), & 1, hopefully, on Miguel Hernandez.

Also just completed *Big Scream* 16 > not one of my best issues, but it has some highlights—Tom Jepsen's translations of Trakl + Heym—will send.

Working hard (2 jobs—janitor & cleaning ghetto apts.); been sick, got my garden in, planning to spend my vacation at Tahquamenon Falls & Painted Rocks in UP Lake Superior—getting away from the metal noise for a while.

I hope you're well. Thanks for getting me together with Andy & Antler last March. First time I'd met Antler—we have a lot in common, Lake Michigan North woods writing base.

Love

Dave

Allen to David　　　　　　　　　　　　　　　　　　　　　　　　　N. Y. June 5, 83

Dear David—I don't have the Follett address, or editor—Anthology sounds good, I'm working with Randy Roark at Naropa on similar *Friction* (his) magazine project, similar + small.

Amiri Baraka—808 South 10th St. Newark N.J. 07003. David Henderson might help—I don't have his address here. After I got copies of *Quiet Lives* thanks—I sent one off to Gordon Ball in Japan to show his students—and one is in the Naropa Library. I'm in N.Y. a few days, thence to W. Virginia for reading, thence to Boulder + Rocky Mt. Dharma Center for monthlong retreat—thence July 13-Aug. 15 to work a week each with Snyder + Creeley—then NY Aug 20-Sept 2—then Naropa thru Fall to Dec—then come back to N.Y. + stay home a year, work on papers—write operas—stare at the moon—

　　　　　　　　　　　　　　　　　Love Allen

P.S. Steve Kowit of San Diego is an interesting poet—don't know his face only a book.
　　　Gregory Corso here writing lots…[garbled]

David to Allen　　　　　　　　　　　　　　　　　　　　　　　　　10/30/83 AG

Hello Allen!
Hadn't heard from you in some time, so I called NYC where Steven gave me your address in Boulder. I have several concerns—first, have you got any new poems of yours you're really crazy about, & where can I get a copy? Mag, books, whatever—My daughter Anne really digs your *First Blues* record; you've got a whole new audience coming up.

Second, am translating Lorca's *Romancero Gitano* with the help of a few friends. This book really turns me on! I came to it with no theories about Lorca's writing, only my natural inclinations & a great love of the Spanish language—&, if I may be pardoned the vanity, I think I'm doing a terrific job of translating. I wonder if you have an address for Bobby Dylan so I could send him a copy when I'm finished.

Third, am mimeographing new *Big Scream*—it's a fair issue, not the hottest, but with some pleasant surprises; & a chapbook, *The Strand*, by Bob Rixon (who you may remember as a disc jockey at WFMU East Orange, who interviewed you re *First Blues*); listen, you may think of me as the inheritor of Reznikoff's energy; this kid lives & breathes Williams, I shit you not. The book has two longer poems, *The Strand* & *The News*, both dealing with New Jersey locale, & with same peculiar Williams-like savvy, ironic, but with a wink. Shorter poems in chapbook show influence of Joel Oppenheimer; I think Rix is one to watch, who's going to grow & one day be a real master. (Well, enough hype—I'll send you chapbook when it's done.)

I read your review of Trungpa's stuff. The review didn't really tell me what he's written about—too much of tradition & higher & lower grade poets, etc.—did he write, say, about the long journey out of Tibet, all the hardships & perils he must've faced with his people? My God, that man must have a story to tell! But did he tell it? (Must confess I've never read any of his works—tho they are definitely on my list of things to get to; I am not one of those younger poets who takes pleasure at sniping at the Buddhists for their success in Boulder, but would rather learn from those whose perspective may be different from mine.)

Also, would have given my eye teeth to be at your Williams birthday celebration in Jersey. Just knowing it happened made my day (have been listening heavily to his 1954 recordings lately while finishing table & chairs in garage, typing mss., etc.. no words to describe my feelings for his voice. Whew!

Enough. It's a clear fall day here in Michigan; I'm alone with the birds singing out the window & the shade-shine playing in the walnut trees. I hope you're well—& Peter as well. I think of you often, & fondly.

Peace

Dave Cope

Allen to David   Naropa 2130 Arapahoe Boulder Colo. 80302   10/30/83 1:30 AM

Dear David: *Vajadhatu Sun* printed only 1/2 my essay. The meatier stuff is in book. Trungpa wrote long narrative autobiog (w. English lady help) *Born in Tibet* which gives adventures + trek across Himalaya. I eliminated the theoretic stuff in book essay, which bored you (+ me) in *Sun* version.

  Send Rixon chapbook or anything else you print. I'm working on 6 page Dream Vision of my mother a sort of epilogue to "Kaddish" 25 years later— "White Shroud," this month. But nothing new published.

  Do you have *Birdbrain* single record? I also made tape of "Jessore Road" with Mondrian string quartet Jan 2 1983 Amsterdam, Steven Taylor conducting his score, me singing. Now I'm reading + teaching Poe, Melville's poems, Emily D. + Walt W. —Allen Ginsberg.

[left sidebar:] *White Shroud* came from reading E. A. Poe complete poesy.

Allen

David to Allen   5 Nov 83 AG

Dear Allen

  I wrote Naropa for a list of Trungpa's books. Where can I get tape of "Jessore Road"? Copy shd also be sent to Bob Rixon for airing on WFMU—he's sure to play it. Address: 322 Mitchell Ave, Linden, N.J. 07036. I've been re-reading all your books, thinking of the big Collected Poems I understand you'll have out next year.

  My two latest pieces're enclosed. The whole Beirut/Grenada business has me really upset—not that I didn't expect this sort of behavior from the present administration, but that so many young boys here in G.R. find in it purpose & adventure, & that once again a blanket of hatred seems to be filling the land. If ever we needed a band like the Beatles to break thru the madness in the media, now is the time—but I see no one on the horizon—Clash too obviously political . . .

Am sending Nada publications under separate cover.

Glad to see you're teaching Melville—his "Ruined Villa" poem is a favorite of mine, also certain of the Civil War pieces. Someone shd be teaching Thoreau again, & Emerson, esp. his "Ode" beginning "Tho loath to grieve," & essay on Self-Reliance as source of spontaneity & 1st thought.

Am now taking a 2 week rest from poetry responsibilities to spread compost leaves on a new 20 X 60 ft area of my garden. City brings me dumptrucks full of leaves free.

All for now. I hope you're well & full of vitality! Will write again later when you're back in NYC.

Peace
Dave

PS. Rix sent me a great tape which has among other things Reznikoff reading his dog story + the poem about the young man who lost his job + offers a cigarette, & the little one about "do not suppose that all who live on 5th Avenue are happy."

Attachment: "Grieving Politicians," a poem later abandoned.

Allen to David   Naropa 2130 Arapahoe Boulder 80302   11/16/83

Dear David:

Rick McMonagle an interesting poet ex-student was here for tea so I loaned him the new *Big Scream* + Rixon's fine pamphlet to read + show around. I've been in touch with Rixon before but not read his writing till you sent it. *Jessore Road* tape I'm still working on but it's not done.

Oy Gevalt! What if they go on to invade Nicaragua! Emerson ode 1846 "Behold the famous states/ Harrowing Mexico/ with rifle and with knife." Now I'm reading through Emily Dickinson. Just back from weekend w/ Kesey's Tibetan lama in Eugene Oregon + reading with "Gregor Samsa" a rock band at Reed College. Guillén's work I don't know well. An older man now wasn't helpful to young Cubans pushed around by Socialist bureaucracy—caught in the middle—Do you know the Portugese turn of century extravagant poet Fernando Pessoa?

—As ever—Allen Ginsberg

David to Allen   Likely from 1983 or 1984

Dear Allen & Peter

Please note a correction in my booklet just sent you. <u>Seven</u> dead in Buffalo, not fourteen. The horror of it is the same; but I'd prefer that the writing be exact.

Dave Cope

David to Allen   after 11/16/83 and before 1/18/84

Dear Allen
a quick one in response to your card. Re Guillén, main beauty of his poem is, for me, immense rhythmic change-ups, as

Tamba, tamba, tamba, tamba,
tamba del negro que tumba

a thumping rhythm that really gets an audience going, dropping into a line with similar sound values yet leading elsewhere. I've used his "Canto Negro" in teaching elementary kids, & while cleaning lunch room at noon, I can shout "Oho!" & they'll respond with his refrain "Yambambó! (Ehe!—Yambambé!" I did this similarly last year with your arrangement of Blake's "Spring," which I used with 1st-4th graders, & had them singing "Merrily, merrily . . ." in lunch room.

Don't know Pessoa's work.

Still no reviews of my book, tho George Tysh arranged for me to read at the Detroit Institute of Art next March. I've got a month vacation next summer—who should I contact for readings in Boulder or San Francisco? I might also go to NYC, think Jimmy Ruggia might be able to help me get something there.

Lanigan is already pressing me to do another book—shit, all I've got is 20 pages of things worth looking at, & I really don't want to hurry it too much, as result is most often shoddy work.

I've never been able to get inside of Emily Dickinson's poems; can you give me some key works to go after? I realize her importance to development, but there's just too damn many poems about bees to continually hold me.

Got my 4th copy of your *Howl* every time I loan it out, I never see it again—this, the 31st printing. Congratulations.

                              Peace
                              Dave Cope

                       Welcome back to NYC
                       to welcome in the year

Allen to David   1/18/84 1 AM

[ordinary script letter inscribed among **bold** words of invitation]

Dear David—Enclosed postcard typescript corrected
one line added to explain West Lake (Park)—
ALLEN GINSBERG
I'll send you a copy of my collected poems
MEMORY GARDENS
SELECTED PHOTOGRAPHS 1953-84
from Harper + Row this week—photo show
been a pleasure—yes Creeley *Mirrors* poems
JANUARY 4-26, 1985
OPENING RECEPTION, SUNDAY, JANUARY 6, 2-5 PM
in China at a dozen universities—No new typescripts
tho I wrote lots in China—Happy New Year—
Holly Solomon Gallery
724 FIFTH AVENUE NEW YORK 10019
212/757-7777

I'll be reading in Detroit (Institute of Arts) c/o Geo Tysh on
Feb 14 + at Flint C.S. Mott College Feb. 15—Love Allen

David to Allen 2-10-84

Hello Allen! Enclosed new *Hall School Poems*—every December & January now I spend 45 minutes in each class, shedding custodial outer skin for professorial wild-eyed teacher pose, & run the gamut of 1st to 6th grades, & here's the result. Next *Big Scream* is nearly full, out in April. I have a really fine reading organized for me by George Tysh at Detroit Institute of Art in March; & my old teachers at local J.C. have asked me to come & lecture on modern poetics, the first reading a real pleasure, I'm really hot & full of energy for this one, & the second a change to read my favorite Pound, Williams, Reznikoff, Ginsberg, Corso & O'Hara poems to my old teachers who confessed they didn't understand what has happened since Eliot (but were willing to learn!)—interspersing readings with "A Retrospect," quotes from Reznikoff's 1969 interview, Williams musings, your letter to Eberhart (izzat still in print? I got it out of library & xeroxed but would like to purchase if. . .), & O'Hara's personism idea.

[Left sidebar in Allen's hand: ask permission to send one + bill me]

Been reading a blue streak, really crazy now about Snyder's *Axe Handles*—DAMN, what a fine text! He should win all the prizes for that! & Michael McClure's *September Blackberries* which I confess I only recently picked up, I love these poems where he stings you with these little couplets rhymed when you least expect it. Also just finished Rexroth's autobiography which despite tiny print, aggravation to this blind bat, was my first non-stop 2 day read in years.

Also busy exercising—I quit smoking—all kinds—& drinking totally for last 6 weeks (tho I indulged with Vietnamese friends over Tet holiday) & am swimming 2 ½ miles a week plus doing leg holds & sit-ups daily. My own poems're coming well—a few samples with this, too.

Rixon sent me a gorgeous tape of Kerouac reading with Steve Allen back-up.

What's kicking in your neck of the woods? Have you seen new Met Museum guidebook, nicely done? Saw your interview in *San Juan Star,* the Void baseball team.

                    Peace
                    David Cope

[Right sidebar vertical line near "the Void": Whazzat??? AG

Attachment: 5 typed poems ("Bucolics," "After the Reading," "Further Progress," "Country Store," "Walking Back to the Car") all but "Further Progress" later abandoned. Handwritten annotation to "Further Progress": "This last perhaps a borrowing from your 'Don't Grow Old' pt. III, unconscious. My poet friend Nate Butler shot in head at a reading he was to give last Dec. here in G. R., now recuperating slowly."

David to Allen   in Allen's hand: 2782 Dixie S.W. Grandville Mich 49418 March 23, 1984

First, thanks for the *Friction.* What can I say? Amazing anthology—I was really glad you brought Katz & Cohn & Ruggia on, among others. I'm imitating your cover for next *Big Scream* & my new chapbook, *On the Bridge* —Bob Rixon's on cover of B.S. & me & Andy on Ruggia's stoop in Hoboken will be on cover of OTB. Will send later—

Didja get my tape from Detroit? Small audience, extremely attentive—no clapping or yowling, thank God, until I had finished. Anyroad I talked to Paul Lichter at Maximus Books & to George Tysh at DIA about getting Andy in there—a reading this summer at Maximus, cheap, probably 50-75 bucks but it's gas money to Boulder; & probably next winter or spring at DIA if he plays his cards right. As you must know, a reading in the art institute is royal treatment, & the money's great; further, great town for Andy to plug his book.

[Left sidebar with arrow to "Didja get my tape": Am sure that Andy could get them jumping—we have different audience preferences, I guess.

I've been busy as hell, please don't mind if I run off at the mouth.

At local J. C. where until last Thursday Eliot still held sway, I introduced 6 great modern poets to college audience, & read directly from the works, selecting my favorites: Pound, Williams, Reznikoff, a short break, then Jack K., you, & O'Hara. You & Reznikoff took the cake, they disliked Pound until I got to "E. P. Ode Pour," liked Williams pretty well, Kerouac's "Western haiku" & I didn't have much time left for O'Hara. Of your work, I read the "Song" (yes yes that's what I always wanted), "Howl" part III, "Returning to the Country" (old one the dog), sang "Father Death"—I did a good job; latter portions of "Plutonian Ode" (starting with "canker-hex on multitudes") + last section, ending with the "Rune" from the "Contest of Bards." I didn't have much time for each poet, & I wanted to give them a taste of your range.

Now reading *Cutting Thru Spiritual Materialism*—& it is exactly what I need now

Swartz stopped in & spent the night—we got on the phone & read Denby & Williams into Ruggia's answering machine—great funny laugh call back later. Man, wait'll you see the 4 poems I got off Swartz for *B.S.*—exact progression beginning with letting himself scream & ending with a great poem, "Dear Jim, Be Gaudy" which he wrote while he was here (great lines about six-legged sestinas, etc.)

I am probably staying in Michigan again this summer. I didn't get all the way up to Painted Rocks on Lake Huron [ridiculous mistake for a Michigan boy—Superior] & Tahquamenon Falls last summer, maybe dis time.

O.K. that's about the whole shot. THANK-YOU, MAN.

Peace

Dave Cope

PS. Your photo of us on *Friction* cover one of the happiest days in this boy's life. Ruggia did PERFECT Review of *QL* in *Home Planet News*.

Allen to David April Fools Day 84

Dear David—
    I wish Randy R. had sense to put twice as many of your poems (which I'd pulled out in the huge fields of empty paper where your (+ Bobby Meyers) poems occupied only the top of the page. Well I wasn't on the spot. He worked so hard I haven't heart to complain tho it thinned down the anthology unnecessarily.
    You sound happily energetic—I'm frantic with unfinished work w Collected Poems + Collected Existence as well.
Short of ink—Allen Ginsberg

David to Allen Apr 23, 84

Dear Allen
Re your question "where do words come from?" which I recall you asking in *Naropa* magazine, Hugh Kenner's *The Pound Era* has an excellent essay "The Invention of Language" that endeavors to find an answer.
    I hope your collected poems will include the poems from Angkor Wat in 'em. > I used to have hardcover edition, somebody stole it.
Peace
David Cope

Now reading Shakespeare's sonnets, I want to write tight in the next 10 years
[Drawing of me in sunglasses, long grass stem w/ hayseed dangling from mouth.]

Allen to David   November 11, 1984 Sunday afternoon

Dear David: hazy in steamer lounge
3'd day down Yangtze River, yesterday
passed vast mountain gorges and hairpin
river-bends, mist sun and cement Factory
soft Coal dust everywhere, all China
got a big allergic cold. Literary dele-
gation homebound after 3 weeks, now I'm
travelling separate like I used to—except
everywhere omnipresent kindly Chinese
Bureaucracy meets me at airports & boats
& takes me to tourist hotels & orders meals. I'm
trying to figure a way out—envious of 2
bearded hippies travelling 4th class in
steerage eating Tangerines & bananas—
sleepers in passageways on mats, Chinese
voyagers playing checkers. Saw Beijing,
Great Wall, tombs & palaces, Suchow's
Tang Gardens, Hangchow's West Lake walkway
dyke to hold the giant water in the years of drought
built by governors of Tsu-Tung-Po and Po-Chu-I.
Saw Cold Mt. Temple w/ Snyder who'd
heard its bell echo across years.
      Love Allen Ginsberg

David to Allen   Nov 84

Dear Allen

Your postcard arrived after performance of Pales Matos' "Danza Negra" for assembled 500 at local Puerto Rican discovery day celebration. Text of postcard is a real clear objectivist piece, could I place it in next *Big Scream?* Or have you something else that I could print therein? Issue #20 already has Clausen's "The Ukrainian Speaks" & Poniewaz's "Whitman in San Francisco," & I have asked Creeley, who sent me an enthusiastic postcard on #19, for something of his. I'll send text of your postcard with this letter, possibly you might want to eliminate letter format & give it a title tho however you'd wish it is OK with me.

Man, what a trip! Ruggia at same time was in Turkey interviewing Afghan refugees, visiting grave of Endymion, pondering Justinian's murder of 50 million, describing reeking post-rain streets of Istanbul & being offered 40 sheep for his wife Sharon, who added that he held out for a better deal [see note]. Will you be in NYC this summer? I'm going to Maryland, thence to Virginia where I want to visit Monticello—have been reading Jefferson's letters, utterly seduced by his sense of purpose & clarity as to future global directions, & I want to walk his rooms & muse on his old farm; then up to Jersey to hopefully hang out with James & Rix & whoever shows up, sing Shelley & Williams & Denby & whoever comes to mind among friends until we're all too tired to keep going—if you're in NYC, I'd love to visit Met or Cloisters or someplace you know where intelligence lies, with you. I'm not sure if I like these big crazy readings where the audience expects the poet to bray like a jackass; have found the simple moments of intelligence with one or two friends are where my directions lie. OK, if you'll be there, please let me know & I'll drop by.

Other—have been reading Trungpa more closely than anybody I've read in a long time, also Lhalungpa's translation of Milarepa book. Am not sure I could ever become a Buddhist per se, but have found these books inspiring. In poetry, nobody right now can hold a candle to Creeley's *Mirrors*, for me; he's been a continual sunshine over the past 8 months.

Welcome back to America!

        Paz
        David

          [in Allen's hand: rc'd & (illegible)
             1/18/85 AG]

Attached: "Lucy," poem about my aunt's life & death, and walking on shore with my father, Signed and dated "Noviembre 84"—later published in my *On the Bridge* **(Humana, 1986).**

David to Allen   Jan 14 1985

Dear Allen
   This is just to invite you to send a poem or two—short, objectivist type, if possible—for the Spring issue of *Big Scream*. I presently have work by George Drury, Paul Mariah, Robert Peters, Joel Lewis, Jeff Poniewaz, myself, & others. Will publish James Ruggia's 1st chapbook simultaneously.
   Am busy—read [from] Blake's *Songs of Innocence & Experience* to Eng Lit class at local college yesterday including rousing acapella version of your tune to "Tyger Tyger"; will videotape my own poems in performance next month, + videotape I made last year is presently being shown to freshman comp students.
   I'm searching for the next generation, no luck so far.

   <My second book to be published this summer—I'll send you a copy.

           David Cope

PS a sad note Paul Mariah tells me Jean Genet has just died—no details yet—have you heard?

Missing letter: Allen's instructions on editing the "postcard poem." (See Allen's script on November 11, 1984, and my letter responding to it with request, November 1984).

David to Allen 1 24 85

Hi Allen
Thanks for instruction on final form of your postcard poem which I'll place in BS 20.
  I'll be in Detroit on Feb 14 to see you, hopefully to get in for 3 o'clock book signing too. My second book *On the Bridge* now fully collated + complete, I'll send to Humana within the week.
           Peace
           Dave

David to Allen Feb 85

Dear Allen
  This is to thank you for allowing me the pleasure of sitting with you as you signed books in Detroit. Also, your reading was excellent; I do worry that you're not getting enough rest.
  I'll mail out other copies of *Big Scream* with your Chinese postcard poem in about a month, when I finish running & collating Jim Cohn's *Divine April*.
  Am now beginning biography of Marpa, companion volume to Milarepa text.
           Peace
           David

Attachment: "New Windows" poem, later published in *On the Bridge*.

David to Allen May 85

  [on yellow lined steno paper]

Dear Allen
  I've been doing extended study of measure as it relates to the "form of the line being commensurate with sentiment of the verse" & wonder if you could give me an adequate definition of "first thought, best thought." Is revision, i.e. as I see it, later perfecting the expression of that first thought—for sometimes the first thought is at first crudely developed—a real possibility within that dictum? Secondly, does "thought" refer to the sentiment alone, or more precisely to the image or movie scenario the poet develops in order to express sentiment?

  Have been reading Campion + Shakespeare (sonnets) who led me back to Petrarch + Dante's *Vita Nuova* (O delicious Italian verse), thence to Provence (found an excellent volume *Lyrics of the Troubadours + Trouveres*, ed. & tr. Frederick Golden with original texts). Am trying to find a way to integrate quantities + Old English stressed line into modern poetical usage, understanding them as *tools* rather than as forms.

Have written a whole batch of new poems I'm proud of. Hope everything's A-OK in your neck of the woods.

With profound respect & wishes for Peace

Love, Dave Cope

Attachment: "Catch" poem later published in *On the Bridge*. At bottom of attached poem: —I invented a tune for "Rose-Cheekt Lawra" & sang it a cappella to students at local Junior College—along with readings of "Eard-Stapa," Chaucer's "Prologue + Donne, + Reznikoff, your "Love Forgiven" + one of Denby's sonnets.

Missing letter from Allen: sending me copyright info on Marsden Hartley's work per following letter.

David to Allen   Oct 85

Hi Allen
    Sorry I won't make it to your reading in A2—no time, making money for Fall publications.
    Thanks for copyright info on Hartley—will pursue.
    Will send Fall *Big Scream* later.
My 2nd book to be publ. by Humana next summer + will catch up to you next time yr in Mich—I miss you.

    Peace Dave Cope

Attachment: "White Sky in Empty Time," poem later abandoned, with hand-scribed query re one line.

Allen to David   2/4/86 6 AM

Dear David,
    Here are 3 poems—finished mss. of *White Shroud: Poems 80-85*, —from latter mss. My agent probably sent them elsewhere but no harm if you print them first in tiny *Big Scream*.
    Also enclosed 2 poems I received in mail from one Chris Ide an odd kid (20? 18?) been writing me from East Lansing. The writing seems straightforward.
    Back from Nicaragua—Marxist one party state halfway, but cheerful + grim, faced w/ U.S.A. thugs—at least freer + more diverse + pluralist than El Salvador where Deathsquads hit the journalists instead of censors

As ever
Allen

Up working all nite trying to answer mail—Ah! ugh! Help!

David to Allen Feb 86

Hi Allen

Will use all yr poems sent in *Big Scream*—especially pleased with "Written in My Dream by W. C. Williams," breathtaking poem, recalls for me Blake's proverb the road to Excess leads to the Palace of Wisdom.

Got some fine work by H. D. Moe in Berkeley, do you know him? Also Antler OK'd "Enskyment" for this issue.

Will correspond with Chris Ide whose poems you sent.

& hello to Crazy Andy Clausen, give your audience the old razzamatazz

>Peace to you both
>+ thanks
>Dave Cope

>relight that fire
>floating in many a lost chord
>on the tortoise shell lyre,
>compassion's touch renewed,
>phantom love restored.

Allen to David Feb. 14, 1986

Dear David:

My agent sent the Williams dream poem to *Poetry* mag, Chicago, where I've never published a poem + they took it but sent form saying it can't have been published in any form before. So don't print that one in *Big Scream*, use the other 2 short poems I sent. I did send 3 (incl. WCW yes? I'd phone you for swiftness but lack your phone number. Forgive the self-referential postcard [photo of Allen], I just got a dozen from Mary Beach [photographer]. How you doing? I've finished *White Shroud* poems 1980-85 in which those poems will be put, working on line-by-line & finished w/ Part I yesterday *Annotated Howl*.

>Love as ever Allen

Re Naropa yes I'll do what I can but Anne Waldman's the boss—write to her.

David to Allen Feb. 86

Superscript: Did you get Nov *Poetry Project Newsletter* with Hartley essay + selection of his work?

Hi Allen

OK will delete Williams dream poem. Congratulations on *Poetry* acceptance. If you have other poems you'd like to place in *Big Scream* will save 2 pages for your work besides page which contains "It's All So Brief" and "No Longer."

My phone number is 616 531 1442.

I wonder, could you send me addresses of 3 poets in USSR, 3 in China & 2 in Nicaragua? I'd especially like to contact poets in China, Ernesto Cardenal, + also Gordon Ball who I think is in Japan. Will send *Big Screams* to whoever you have addresses for. I think is important too that others realize humble mimeo scene exists here in USA. Also to stimulate cultural exchange if possible.

Also I wanted to query you as to whether I might teach in summer session at Naropa in a year or two? I could sing Campion & do readings of Blake, or objectivists if you prefer <[sidebar] could do bangup readings of WCW. Have learned Campion's tunes by listening to recent releases of his poems, & composed a tune of my own for "Rose Cheekt Lawra." Also wd like to meet Mr. Trungpa—have assiduously studied texts—biographies of Marpa + Milarepa, Trungpa's own *Born in Tibet, Cutting Through Spiritual Materialism* & *Myth of Freedom* as well as Osel Tendzin's *Buddha in the Palm of Yr Hand*.

Lately experimenting with telescoping technique Williams used on pages 54-55 of *Paterson* also found in many renaissance paintings wherein main action + subject happens before extended landscape backdrop that may or may not be concerned with the main action—see notebook poem enclosed, "Ice Storm Procession."

OK all for now. Write soon Let the Renaissance begin again!

Paz David Cope

Attached poems: "The Garden in Winter," "At the Elevator" (typed ms.) and "Ice Storm Procession" (handwritten ms.), all eventually abandoned.

David to Allen   note in Allen's hand: arriv'd 3 24 86. Mars 86

Dear Allen

Tom Lanigan asks if is OK I could use enclosed photo of you + me for back cover of my 2nd book On the Bridge.

Also I'll be in Boulder July 15 to read in Andy Clausen's series. Any chance I could do a Monday July 14 reading or lecture at Naropa? I could do an *Excellent* reading-lecture on Stieglitz-Hartley-WCW "roots of objectivist tradition" & relate it to what I'm trying to do now—for nominal fee 2 hours for $100 + opportunity to meet Trungpa on 12th or 13th July (will be in Boulder Sat 12th thru Tues 15th).

Sidebar: [in Allen's hand: Anne—yes!—can we?—Allen
          PEACE NICARAGUA
                              Dave
PS: A new world's only a new Mind Eternity's in love with the Productions of Time

Attachment: Loose manuscript poem "After the Reading, a Party" dated Jan 1986, possibly accompanying following letter of Mars (March) 86.

David to Allen   3 March 1986

Dear Allen
　　　　No need to send more poems to *Big Scream*—have now completed production of mag, will mail out in 2-3 weeks.
　　　　Now reading Horace—first U of Chicago translations then originals—afraid my Latin's pretty rusty. Steven Taylor still making a record of Horace's poems with guitar?

Paz
David Cope

Allen to David   3/24/86

Dear David: of course you can use the photo—I only wish there were one in which we're both standing up straight without a flashbulb (it looks like)—Antler's book is great looking, amazing! —congratulations on yours—Allen

Allen to David   4/7/86 1:30 AM N.Y.C.

Dear David—
　　　　I did send you 3 poems did you get them? Re yr card 3 March—I've been away so didn't read it till now.
　　　　Yes Steven set several Horace songs, but not recorded them. He's working w/ Sanders (Ed) on *Star Peace* opera, + with Kenward Elmslie, and me, + others. How's yr book coming. Did you contact Anne for Naropa? Did you see Antler's *Last Words* (Ballantine?)—

Love Allen G.

[right sidebar:] Just read your Feb. 86 letter I've been away—will answer later. —railroad roundhouse / wears a wreath of fog is classic.

David to Allen   14 Avril 86

Hi Allen
Yes you sent me 3 poems; then later asked that I not publish one, "Written in My Dream by WCW" [,] wonderful poem, because *Poetry* wanted to publish that one on condition it not be published elsewhere. I agreed; & published only the 2 shorter pieces, "It's All So Brief," & "No Longer." Will send you more copies of the magazine if you need them.

I wrote Anne about lecturing at Naropa but she said no $$ were available & also it was "Women's Week" the week I'd be in Boulder. I wrote back & sd I'd be pleased just to be there & see everybody. *Would* like to hold an open reading at Andy's so students can show me what they're doing; would also like to climb Mt. Audubon or Long's Peak; & if possible, I'd like to meet Mr. Trungpa. (& see you again if yr not too busy).

Antler sent me autographed *Last Words*: "To Brother Poet of Inland Ocean Realms—May we live to be old men / and laugh"—touched me. I like to think of me + Andy + Antler as old men together at some future poesy conference unravelling the traditions for kids who'll carry torches to generations unborn even then.

My book's being typeset now. Thanks for kind comments on "railroad roundhouse wears a wreath of fog." If I don't see you this summer (hope I do!), perhaps will see you this fall.

Thought-clouds pass overhead
& are gone
I pass you back the Peace
You've taught me to find

David

PS Kids like Chris Ide in E. Lansing better prepare for hard choices re draft/war resistance etc. I think we're in for another round of Hell on Earth soon

Peace

Let all the artists + poets + musicians get together again
Will be in Boulder July 13-July 17   In Allen's hand: illegible 4/18/86.

Allen to David   4/18/86 N.Y.C.

Dear David:
Yes I'll be in Boulder July 13-17 and if I have a class you can teach it and I'll pay you. I got more fine poems from Chris Ide. Got Antler Ballantine; can't seem to get any help for Clausen, maybe his mss. needs an unmessy editor. —well, soon—Allen

[right sidebar:] Tell Humana to send new book to Amer. Academy c/o Lydia Karin [uncertain; check name]

David to Allen   Apr 30 86

Dear Allen
Thanks for your offer to let me address your class at Naropa. Teachers at local J. C. where I am janitor found out I was coming to Naropa + gave me their classes for a day to help me raise money for trip. I can't wait to get out there & see everybody!
    Spent 3 days on Big Manistee River, canoed old Marquette exploration route, my tent visited nightly by deer herds.

Paz

Dave Cope

PS Have gotten a real kick out of this Chris Ide you sent me—guess he'll be at Naropa too.

David to Allen 6 18 86

Hi Allen

First THANKS for the most peaceable & dignified 4 days I've had in years.

I wrote review of Antler's *Last Words* & shot it off to *Poetry Flash*. Also wrote Paul Mariah to alert him + others of Antler's visit & asked for other review outlets in S. F. if *Poetry Flash* doesn't want it.

Jim Cohn has been made Editor of *Writers & Books Newsletter* in Rochester, so eventually review will be published there if none of these West Coast mags take it.

Several A-1 poems came from Boulder experience. I ordered Cendrars book—thanks.

Look forward to seeing you again next summer, Objectivist Fiesta

Paz
David Cope

PS Send any short objectivist type new poems you've got. Have decided to do another *Big Scream*.

David to Allen Sunday morn Aug 3 86
[in Allen's hand: Cadillac Squawk OK sent 8/9/86]

Dear Allen + Steve

First, if either of you have short poems for *Big Scream*, please send 'em. Steinbeck sent me his "Palindrome on Impermanence," Mariah sent me a poignant "Death Ode" & I have gorgeous short poems from Antler + Jeff, all for this issue.

Am working on getting a grant for reading series in G. R. What's your current fee for readings?

Steven, I want to thank you + Ed for new Fugs album, which I have thoroughly enjoyed. I have suggestion for your next album: perhaps (if you can't attract a record company to do a complete album of Horace's songs) you could pick a favorite + slip it into the next Fugs record. Have you set Ode II.3 ("Aequam memento rebus in arduis") to music? (One part of me says, "don't keep bothering Steven about this", but another part keeps saying "how would it sound in my ears?" & surely your scholarship + efforts deserve reward, as well.

Am busy now with Virgil's *Eclogues*. Ruggia is sending me Basil Bunting's poems, which I've never read, & I have ordered Blaise Cendrars' *Postcards from America*. Hartley's *Complete* due out in September!

OK   Fee should include cost of 1 reading
Peace   + 1 lecture on subject of your choice
David Cope

[in Allen's hand: Poem sent—Cadillac Squawk 8/9/86 AG]

David to Allen 8 11 86

Dear Allen

    Thanks for your "Cadillac Squawk" for *Scream* 23.
    Best issue yet shaping up, esp if I can get Clausen, Ruggia + Creeley.

    Onward Maestro!

                       Paz

                       David

David to Allen 8 24 86

Dear Allen

    My *On the Bridge* will be out in November. Do you know anyplace I could get a reading in NYC during that time, and if I can get a reading, could I stay at your place? (Assuming you'll be in NYC during that time).
    Back cover has your recommendation along with kudos from Creeley, Rakosi, Ruggia & George Drury. I'll make sure you get copies.
    Chris Ide's been coming over weekly—pleasant kid, a lot of good discussion. His new poems more introspective into his place in the world as a gay man.
    OK all for now.

                       Peace
                       Dave Cope

Missing letter from Allen (with advice re my manuscript collections and Paragon House opportunity).

David to Allen 14 Dec. 1986

Dear Allen

    Thanks for advice re my manuscript collections + also info re Paragon House. I neglected to ask you how Trungpa is doing—I hope he is well. I passed his *Spiritual Materialism* book to Chris Ide + hope the kid'll pick up on it. Also hope Peter is well + that you have happy Christmas Hanukkah New Years et al. Next year you & I & others will bring a whole new generation alive to Williams + Reznikoff, what a pleasurable task!
                       Peace Dave

David to Allen 1 29 87

Superscript: Ph 616 531 1442—Naropa wrote me, said you didn't have my phone number.

Dear Allen

    Did you get my *On the Bridge*?—my publisher was supposed to send you one.

I hope you're well—not enough time to really enjoy time with you when I saw you in Lansing tho you made wonderful impression on my friend Bill who is slowly dying of ALS.

Could you send me Galway Kinnell's address? I'm writing prose book for Paragon House + want to promote works of Clement Marot, du Bellay + Ronsard—important part of tradition neglected this cy.—Kinnell did excellent translations of Villon & I wondered if he'd be interested in these others or if he had specific take on their works.

Poem enclosed my most recent.

Chris Ide went to San Francisco, I miss the kid but he had to find his way.

Write if so inclined. See you next summer.

Peace Dave Cope

Attached poem: "Sky Spread Out With Stars," one of the birth poems for my daughter Jane, later published in *Fragments from the Stars.* **(Humana, 1990).**

David to Allen 2 3 87

Hi Allen

Rec'd your marvelous *White Shroud* in the mail yesterday, only 2 days after writing you re my own book. The China poems stand out right away, along with the title poem—your reading of "White Shroud" with string quartet backing, last summer, was one of the most moving performances I've seen in last 20 years. I have your "Do the Meditation Rock" on tape, recorded off TV on New Year's Day 1984.

OK *thanks* for the whole volume, you shd be mighty proud of it!

I've been busy—read old English "Eard-Stapa," sections of Chaucer's "Prologue" & Skelton's dyties + his "Upon a Deedman's Head" to sophomore English class, who later wrote me big thank-you for spirited performance; was mocked in local press "College Janitor Waits for the Day When Poetry Will Pay" tho reviews praised the poems themselves; good correspondence with Chris Funkhouser, who's written a credible imitation of "Howl" strophes without hydrogen jukeboxes; Ruggia in Istanbul writes of camel wrestling matches + arguments with British lit professors. More later.

Affectionately,

David Cope

Allen to David N.Y.C. 2/4/87

Dear David—*On [The] Bridge* arrived, not yet time to read thru. Kinnell 432 Hudson St. N.Y. N.Y. 10014. Sent you 2 books *Shroud* + *Howl*. Bklyn College term began yesterday, I'm buried under mountain of paper—mail, photos, mss. untyped, I'll shut up awhile. Yours as ever

Allen Ginsberg

[right sidebar:] Sky spread stars interesting mind-mix

David to Allen   Mars 31 87

Dear Allen

Thanks for your Annotated *Howl* book. I don't think Joel Lewis's review in *St. Mark's* did it full justice; I saw it more as a workbook on method & was gratified to see notes bringing language to its sources. Also to have Carl's "Report from the Asylum," your letter to Eberhart + his "West Coast Rhythms," Pound's letter to Williams, the letters re printing the book correctly, the letter from John Hollander, Ferlinghetti's excerpt from "Horn on Howl" etc. all under one cover—*yassuh!* You once wrote a piece called "Poetry, Violence & the Trembling Lambs" which I think I saw in *A Casebook on the Beats* (Parkinson?)—I've never seen elsewhere & wonder if it shd see print again. If you like, I could print in new *Big Scream* due out Jan. 1988. [Sidebar in Allen's hand: send to Cope 1959 S. F.]

I'm busy—wife Sue had a baby girl in March; I designed & am building a solar greenhouse in backyard; reading Hesiod, Rexroth's translations from *Greek Anthology*, new *Collected Hartley* (finally! Wonderful resurrection, after 42 years out of print!), & doing a symposium for elementary students "how to write from the heart."

Am looking forward to Naropa summer session. Jacqueline Gens tells me I'll be staying with you—I wonder if I could impose on you + ask if young poets could visit 1 or 2 evenings & read their poems to me in relaxed living room atmosphere? I want them to have the benefit of my ear, as well as the lecture/readings I'll give them. [Side note in Allen's hand: OK]

                         OK
                       Peace

                     Dave Cope

Allen to David   4/17/87

Dear David—I'll see if I can xerox the essay (originally *S.F. Chronicle*) + send you. Outdated therein last paragraph perhaps. Jackie Gens asked if you could stay in my Varsity apartment a week while you're there I said OK, & OK to have people over. I have other people coming in and out to stay with me other weeks—assuming Peter Orlovsky doesn't come to Naropa in which case he'll need the room all summer + we'll have to make other arrangements. Trungpa died 7:05 this last Saturday

                                     As ever—Allen

David to Allen   6 12 87

Dear Allen

I've prepared the following poems to read for Rakosi lecture you + I are to share: (*Collected Poems*)

                     Services   p. 127
                     Instructions to the Player   139

Lord What is Man?	21
If One Could Write	24
No One Talks About This	26
Man at Work	48

———

The Husband	93
Young Girl	107
The Dead Father	125

———

In What Sense I Am I	134

———

The Senior Citizen	167

———

The China Policy	197
A New Breed	213
"And what were the poets . . ."	299
The Dream	295

———

From *Americana*:

"lies in a glass"	319
GPC	326
Origin of the Blues	335
1924	337
New Orleans Transient Bureau	338
Coca Cola Sign	350
Captain Patterson	357
Simplicity	359

———

8 Meditations	p. 483ff

———

    Is there anything I should know (re your preparations for same lecture) that would make it easier to integrate our presentation?

———

By all signs I hear, a lot of good folks are coming to conference.

                    Peace
                    Dave Cope

David to Allen 7 6 87

ALLEN   [In Allen's hand: 930 5265 / 689 5329 home > Phyllis Segura]

—Call Vicky (nothing urgent)

Also here is key to apt. Thank-you again for good times, hospitality + honest critique. Keep in touch, I'll do same.
Dave Cope

PS: Goodbye to Steven, great memorable night singing Dowland et al, warm memory for winter nights.

David to Allen 1987 Aug 3

Dear Allen

Thanks for sending me Andy Pawelczak's work—I too find it interesting tho may not be able to work it into next *Scream*—mag is full already. I'll write him + perhaps begin correspondence if he's interested.

OK *thanks* for lovely evenings + mornings in Boulder. Steve Silberman has sent me good poems, & both he & Keith Bernstein have begun correspondence. They're together now in S. F. as Ide & Funkhouser are together in Va. Jim Cohn wrote me from Cadillac Ranch, Texas—he'll be here in a few weeks.

I hope Peter is well. I saw your heart was aching but didn't know how to reach out except by doing dishes.
Dave

PS Don't try to do too much—you'll fall on the stairs.

Attached poem manuscript: "Big Manistee April," published in *Fragments from the Stars*. (Humana, 1990).

Allen, Chris Funkhouser, and Chris Ide to David

[Joint undated letter from Chris Funkhouser, Chris Ide, and Allen]

Hi Dave walked to the top o' the cape w/ Steve Silberman last week, now with Chris Ide & Allen in N.Y.C. Lots of fun in recording studio w Fugs & in Central Park & Brooklyn. Will write more soon—Funkster

Hello Dave—will be in N.Y. till Sat., then to E. Lansing, Grand Rapids, will phone—N.Y. is nuts but I'm sober & soakin it up. All ya love—Chris

boys are ok here; Peter is silent & on the fence, can't tell what'll happen. Chris Ide read thru 1000 pages Antler Boy Love poems mss. I'm still limping from Boulder fall. No new poems. Saw Dali w/ big bomber joint in dream. —Allen Ginsberg

David to Allen 8 28 87

Hi Allen

  Postcard from you & Ide & Funk made my day after hard long day serving the professors. I look forward to seeing the boys, love their innocent Energy, did they ask you questions about shewing "that much suffering" in Jack's *Big Sur*? I said, Jack's way to illustrate 1ˢᵗ Noble Truth & also warning, be careful the way you tread.

  Do you & Steve know Coperario's song at end of Campion's *Somerset Masque*, "Come ashore, come merrie mates, with your nimble heels & pates"? *Lovely* song! I'll sing it to you & teach you tune & bet you'll sing it too, next time we meet.

  To Peter: be well, let the stars return to your eyes. I missed seeing you in Boulder, maybe next time.

  Jim Cohn's back in Rochester after SW summer travels, Rixon's going to publish a chapbook himself. Steve Silberman sent me some fine work. *Big Scream* in January 88.

  OK all for now. I'll send you some hot stuff with this & also a memento from our sojourn in Boulder together.

      Respectfully & with Love

        Dave Cope

Attached poems: "Waking Dreams," "Pictures" (two old poets here are Allen & Carl Rakosi), both poems abandoned later.

David to Allen 10 30 87

Hi Allen

  I'll call & confirm re Brooklyn College Springtime reading this weekend:
  1. $300 is plenty (if you can't swing that, call me 616 531 1442).
  2. Any date you can fit me in from March on thru May. Please let me know ASAP

OK enclosed pertains to 2 classes I gave this past month.

---

   1. Intro: Imagist Manifesto
       Jack's Belief + Technique for Modern Prose
       Your 13 Steps for Revising
       Your Different Considerations in Mindful Arrangement

    — "13 Modes of Composition" explained w examples

  2. Overview tracing European lyric tradition w readings & a cappella singing.

Am now teaching Eng 101 (rhetoric + research paper) in night school.
  Big Scream in January

  Paz David

Attachments: **HANDOUT FOR LOCKWOOD'S THURSDAY CLASS** and chart of **GROWTH OF LYRIC TRADITION IN EUROPE**

David to Allen   c. Dec. 87

Dear Allen
Is there any chance Steve Taylor will be in town on the weekend I'll be there/ i.e. April 18? I'd like to do several English renaissance songs as part of my set, & thought perhaps Steve (& you as well, if you're interested) might want to sing & play with me.

I'll do the following songs:

  Where the Bee Sucks, by Robert Johnson (*The Tempest*)
  O Mistress Mine (from *Twelfth Night*)
  It was a lover and his lass (from *As You Like It*)
  Away with these self-loving lads, by John Dowland
  Come again! Sweet love doth now invite, by John Dowland
  Fire! Fire! By Thomas Campion
  Never Weather-Beaten Saile, by Thomas Campion
  Come a shore, come, merrie mates by Giovanni Coperario

OK I'm excited about this trip, the chance to see old friends & make new ones, & to finally be able to sing these songs & work with the era I've found most interesting these past 2 years.

             Peace
             Dave Cope
[right sidebar, in Allen's hand: Steve 12/3/87 I phoned—He'll use this or part in class. AG]

David to Allen   1 15 88

Dear Allen
  Here's yr copies of new *Big Scream* with your famous little essay, poems from last summer's Boulder crowd, poems from poets you sent me, & poems that just appeared in my mailbox.
  Am busy as ever—rehired to teach college research paper writing, finished this mag, 2/3 thru my 3rd book (which Humana has already agreed to publish), looking forward to NYC in April & I just turned 40 this week.

I hope you're feeling fine, & Peter is well. Hello to NY crowd, especially Bob Rosenthal & Steven Taylor.

      Peace
      Dave Cope

David to Allen   2 5 88

Dear Allen
Any chance one of your interns could assemble a manuscript of poems from students in class I'll be addressing in April, & send ms. on to me? I'd like to evaluate their work, maybe begin a conversation by mail with a few of the brighter or more talkative ones handwritten: especially those talented + serious about poesy career].

I'm busy—teaching a night school class; reading yours & Jack's & WCW's & Reznikoff's poems as well as work by Wilfred Owen, Pound & O'Hara to sophomore English classes as guest speaker; still working my janitor/dock manager position; translating Du Bellay's *Antiquities de Rome*—some of these, & reading his *Defense et Illustration de la Langue Française*. I love his wicked wit, turning back on the hungry ghosts:

    Tell me this—for some of you
    may still hide here below—
    does your pain grow greater

    when sometimes, on these Roman slopes,
    you contemplate your own works
    & see nothing more than a dusty plain?

(#15, *A of R*).
Also, I fucked up my leg pushing a 300 lb. cart up receiving ramp; many visits to industrial veterinarian doctors, looks like it'll finally be OK.
              Dave Cope

Allen to David Letter prepping me for visit to his Brooklyn College classes 2/14/88

Dear David—The class of 20 or so are undergrads not writing students. You can stay on past 4:30 to join me in 5:30-8:00 workshop but they bring new poems in each week and I improvise.

    Hope your leg improves.
  I think I sent you reading poster + syllabus by now for lecture class we'll do together on living poets.
      OK—
    Just back from Israel
     —Allen
Rc'd *Big Scream* w Peter Hale photo—I think charming—any problems?

David to Allen   2 19 88

Hi Allen

I wangled another day off from work, so I'll be able to stay on & visit your evening writing workshop as you mentioned.

Am especially interested in meeting those in undergrad class with real future scholarly intentions—either re objectivist tradition or greater poetical history. In your writing workshop, I'd want to meet & yak with the most talented poets. & if possible, before going to NYC, thru mail—poets, to help them towards print & set them on the road, & for friendship's sake; scholars, to grow old sharing peculiar esoteric findings. Students who're interested can write me ahead of time—I'll send *Big Scream* free & give good correspondence. They should ask good questions.

Other—I'd like to fly into NYC on Saturday April 16 & stay at your place, if that's OK. Dave Roskos has a reading lined up for me in New Brunswick on the 17th; he or his friends will provide me transportation to & from. If you're not too busy, come on along; Bob Rixon, Mike Pingarron & possibly Ruggia will be on same bill. Will depart AM of the 19th.

Big Scream cover photo's been hailed by all who've seen it, gay & straight poets alike giving kudos on the tenderness of the pose.

My leg's better.

If Steven's still interested or isn't too busy, I'd love to do some ancient songs with him. Your description of my time with students sounds as tho you'd like me to talk about Objectivists or Whitman—can do, if that's what you prefer.

& Duncan is dead, who showed me *The Golden Bough*, *The White Goddess*, & *The Golden Ass*. Praised be he in passing, who sang fair the lady & her knight, whose Monarchs soared beyond *Caesar's Gate*, Master Poet whose eloquence left me speechless.

Paz
Dave Cope

Hello to Peter.   [in Allen's hand: illegible. . . in letter 2/23/88]

Allen to David   **Second letter prepping me for his Brooklyn College classes**   2/23/88

Dear David—
    Did you receive syllabus & reading poster? That gives you outline what's being taught + in what sequence—yet teach your own poetry + the poetry that you feel akin to by taste + historical circumstance, especially yr predecessors + friends as indicated. The class folk are often intelligent but not widely read, this is an intro to poetry not a superscholarly one, but at least a

80

live class. I'm not sure who in class of 20 or so have "Real future scholarly intentions," there might be a few, if you ask, but they may be too young to decide—it's not like the gang of spiritual desperadoes at Naropa.

      Yes that's fine April 16-19. I leave for a week at Naropa Tues the 9th, also. I do like that *Big Scream* cover too.

      OK thanks—received your pamphlet of poems also—

Allen

David to Allen   March 25 88

Dear Allen
I want to publish Billy Burroughs Jr.'s work in an anthology of poets my generation, but lack address of whoever may hold rights to his works. Could you help me on this—Andy Clausen suggested you might know.

Anthology will contain: Antler, Robert Borden, Burroughs Jr., Janet Cannon, Andy Clausen, Jim Cohn, Myself, Eliot Katz, Michael Pingarron, Jeff Poniewaz, Bob Rixon, James Ruggia, Al Sgambati, John Steinbeck Jr. (also need his address, if you have it?), Tom Swartz, Nina Zivancevic, Elizabeth Kerlikowske. I'll publish it in an edition of 1000 copies, perfect-bound. It'll be 144 pages, & be celebration of 15 years of small press publishing, the 25th issue of my *Big Scream*.

Anyroad, I really want to put Burroughs Jr.'s work in there—taken from work that was published in *New Blood*—but need permission from relatives, spouse, or whoever's responsible for his work. Can you help me?

Dave Cope

Also if Eileen Myles is interested I'd like to publish her work—she shd send 15 pages of work—preferably shorter stuff.

David to Allen   Undated [4 2 88]

Xerograph of *Grand Rapids Press* article from April 2, 1988: "Poet Mops Up: JC teacher-janitor David Cope wins $5,000 grant," by Said Deep. A3-A4.

Handwritten note to Allen in lower right corner: Allen—thought you might enjoy this. See you in a couple weeks. Dave I wrote Burroughs as per our phone talk Friday—

David to Allen   88

Superscript in Allen's hand: Bob read [crossed out / "done"], show Steven, & file.

Hi Allen
      Enclosed 2 poems based on view out yr kitchen window—thought you'd enjoy

Thanks for Brooklyn—

Enclosed Ruggia book has "Psalm #1", p. 25

His influences, among others, Shelley & Byron, Denby, Basil Bunting—

OK see you later. Hello to Peter & Vicki & Bob & Vicki

                        Peace

                        Dave Cope

Attached poems: "Between Buildings" and "Windows," the first of these a draft for the final version found in *Fragments from the Stars*, 66. (1990). The second was abandoned, though there is another New York windows poem in that volume, which may have been written about the same time, though with more overt sexual content: "All These Thousands of Windows," page 73.

David to Allen   1988 Sept. 12

Dear Allen
Possible poesy conference at Naropa 1990 or 1991—earth theme, including farmers, American Indians, atmospheric scientists & Earth First/Planet Drum type activists.

Would also like to include at least one good Buddhist teacher.

These suggestions came from myself, Gary Snyder, Jim Cohn, Antler & Jeff, & my publisher Tom Lanigan.

Is there anybody you think should be added?
I haven't contacted anybody on the list yet, except Anne Waldman—who said to develop the idea & get back to her later—idea is that I'd like input of all of the above plus you, then go back to her. If no dice at Naropa, perhaps somebody else will be interested in conference—I think it's an idea that's long overdue.

OK, I assume you're probably as busy as ever. If this request presumes too much, please put it aside & get your sleep.

                        Paz en Corazon
                        David

PS: *Nada Poems* anthology end of this mo. When's your record coming out?

Attached: "Rainy Dawn," signed and dated Labor Day 1988, later published in *Fragments from the Stars*. (Humana, 1990). Pages 64-65. Also, "EARTH POESY CONFERENCE preliminary groundwork 9-88 2nd revision" (reproduced here, below), plus original letter to Anne Waldman 6-88—enclosed—for possible connections to be made.

Attachment: EARTH POESY CONFERENCE

Preliminary groundwork: 9-88 second revision

PURPOSE

to bring people together to exchange ideas, in the context of earth-based, environmentally active poesy. As many of the participants as possible should be poets, but that is no prerequisite. (Please see original letter to Anne Waldman—enclosed—for possible connections to be made)

PARTICIPANTS

Steve Schneider
Climate Change
National Center for Atmospheric Research
P.O. Box 3000
Boulder, Colorado 80303

Expert on ozone layer damage, greenhouse effect, nuclear winter Several books, including *The Genesis Strategy*, which talks of the "need for nations to take long-term view particularly with respect to food supplies in light of uncertain weather conditions." Recommended by Tom Lanigan.

Wendell Berry
Port Royal, Kentucky

Poet farmer; also activist on behalf of small farmers (see interview in Spring '88 Southern Exposure.) Recommended by both Jim Cohn & Tom Lanigan.

Kenneth Boulding
Department of Economics
University of Colorado
Boulder 80309

Economist at U of Colorado, possibly emeritus now. Could speak re economic distortions of defense-based budgets.

Elise Boulding
(same address)

Radical feminist social scientist contrib. socioecological sphere.

Dhyani Ywahoo
c/o Sunray Meditation Society
P.O. Box 308
Bristol, Vt. 05443

Cherokee teacher. Author, *Voices of Our Ancestors*. Weaves notions common to Native peoples & Buddhists together well.

Joy Harjo
English Department
University of Colorado
Box 226
Denver, Colorado 80309

Native American poet suggested by Tom Lanigan

Dave Forman
c/o Earth First!
P.O. Box 5871
Tucson, Az. 85703

On college circuit; former Sierra lobbyist to speak on split in environmental movement: "Deep" vs "Humanist" ecology. Recommended by Antler & Jeff; Cohn concurs.

Peter Berg
451 30th St.
S. F. Cal.

Planet Drum Foundation Raise the Stakes bioregionalism / "most appropriate" recommended by J. C.

Gary Snyder
18442 Macnab Cypress Road
Nevada City, Ca. 95959

Master eco-poet; busy in summers but "it's possible."

Greg Keeler
English Department
Montana State U.
Bozeman Montana 59715

Keeler is recommended by Gary Snyder, sings and has cassettes out from Earth First! Also "3 great books of poems out too"—GS

Antler & Jeff Poniewaz
1711-A E. Belleview Place
Milwaukee Wisconsin 53211

Antler & Jeff have suggested 6 different themes for their lecture topics, ranging from eco-visions of Thoreau & Whitman to "Poets can help inspire the end of the war against the earth as poets did against Vietnam in the 60s."

Jim Cohn
Birdsfoot Farm
Star Route Box 138
Canton NY 13617

Cohn is a veritable fountain of information, bibliographies, addresses, re this theme. He is currently preparing two lectures for this conference.

Anne Waldman
Naropa

Diane Diprima [sic]
231 Collingwood
S. F. 94114

Bernadette Mayer
172 East 4th St. Apt 9B
NYC 10009

Allen Ginsberg

P. O. Box 582
Stuyvesant Station
NYC 10009

Nanao Sakaki
(reach thru GS—no permanent address)

David Cope
2782 Dixie SW
Grandville Mi 49418

Attachment : Letter to Anne Waldman 6-88

6-88
[in Cope's hand: Original vision]

Dear Anne,
I'd like to outline the Earth poetry conference I spoke to you about the other day, projected for 1991 at Naropa—preliminary groundwork here, with request for your input:

I'm thinking of bringing 4 basic groups together for exchange of ideas:
    Shamans
    Poets
    Earth scientists/ecologists
    Old digger "free" culture.

SHAMANS

    A. AMERICAN INDIAN CHANTS & BLESSINGS
    —enlist local & other (Sioux, Navajo, West Coast, Great Lakes?) Indian medicine people to perform rituals & explain source material, basic mental attitudes in Indian old ways culture.

    B. BUDDHIST CHANTS & BLESSINGS
    —perhaps Buddhists & Indians could develop a dialogue or symposium to locate where they connect with each other.
    —perhaps discussion of how sounds can be used to invoke peacefulness in the spirit (or vice-versa), & thus make us all aware of the subtleties of sound & silence.
    —perhaps performances of Tibetan bowls & bells.
    —other dialogue—discussion based on what arises.

POETS

    A. Poets to select from their works & activities to shew connection of the word to earth, to "the old ways," etc.
    —1 reading & 1 lecture each, plus interviews with students

B. Poets I'd invite: (suggest others)
Snyder
Ginsberg   additions in Cope's hand: :
Sakaki
Sanders
Poniewaz

also in Cope's hand:

DiPrima
Wendell Berry
Waldman   ?
Mayer
Cope
?Zivancevic
Antler
Cohn
Naropa staff
—others?

EARTH SCIENTISTS / ECOLOGISTS

1 speaker each / people with technical backgrounds but also with ability to explain data in layman's terms
—ozone future / greenhouse effect
—nuclear storage—problems of waste cleanup
—economics of defense-based budgets
—developing alternatives in our own lifestyles to clean up our own acts.
—growing infrastructure of resource recovery, & how to nurture it in your own hometown

I have already talked, as of this writing, with local environmental group; there are several speakers' bureaus we can work with to get speakers. Many of the speakers are high-priced by poetry standards, but can be persuaded to come cheaply if the project is presented to them in the correct light. I think adequate press coverage will be a necessity in order to attract these people. Some include Barry Commoner; Stuart Udall, Sister Margene Hoffman (Buffalo—Love Canal), and others.

DIGGER FREE CULTURE (crossed out) / ENVIRONMENTAL ACTIVISTS

These people, or as many as we can get of this group, to speak on their current concerns. I think it important that we are not interested in a 60s nostalgia trip, but in their perceptions of where we are now.

My interest in them is primarily centered in their clear-headed approach of Thoreau-like lifestyle, appropriate technology, & straightforward honest social criticism.

—people I'd invite: [crossed-out: Peter Coyote, Allen Cohen (of "Oracle"), Irving Rosenthal; handwritten note in Cope's hand: see later / Rework as per Antler + Jeff suggestions]
    Abbie Hoffman
    Ponderosa Pine
—possible group discussions: [crossed-out: Hoffman, Rosenthal & Cohen on "media" & "profession" and Hoffman, Pine & Coyote on playfulness.]

Hopefully representatives of each of the 4 groups will be present during the entire conference. I think each approach to the old ways & to earth nurturing can & ideally will give perspective to those working in neighboring fields. Secondly, I think it important to begin the process of interaction among these groups anew—to replant the seeds of clean & upright living in human consciousness at the beginning of the century's final decade.

COSTS

Anne, I'd like to discuss this with you later; my primary concern in this letter is to see if the notions I've developed here are consistent with what you'd like to do in 1991. I do think that, regarding budgets, higher-priced participants should consider foregoing some of their usual fees in order to emphasize the *economy* of this conference & also the importance of its purpose. (This may not of course be feasible, but I'd like your advice on such matters when discussion is appropriate).

I do suggest that Naropa plan a media blitz similar to that mounted for the Kerouac Conference—the ideas we'll develop here are precisely those that most need to be disseminated widely. I think this could be accomplished at minimal cost, enlisting student & other volunteers to disseminate materials & make connections.

OK, that's what I have so far.

Other: there's a kid named Joel Kuszai who'll be coming out within the next few days; he'll stay with Chris Ide for about 3 weeks. Student poet—has a lot of travelling to do in order to arrive at what he wants from his writing—but is a whiz on computer layout, printing & design. If Naropa has MacIntosh computers, you might want to enlist this kid's help in teaching the students or staff in how to do desktop publishing.

[*Nada* Poems] Anthology is hung up on a few small details right now. I think you'll be pleased when you see it.

                                Peace

Dave Cope

Chris Funkhouser to Allen from David's house in Grandville 9 13 88 3 A.M.

Allen—

Here in Grandville just for one night, on my way back to California with my brother—up late now perusing nifty manuscripts & proofs of upcoming NADA anthology, strewn about this lively house (cats, dogs, & 6 people tonight!).

Saw Niagara Falls today for the first time—whatta sight! The power of water! Will be seeing Black Hills, Flatirons, Zion, & Vegas (ick) later this week, & Clausen's reading in SF Sunday so I'll be hurrying in order to get back in time—

Hope all is going well at Brooklyn & at home, will drop you a line when I have new address out west

Much love & best wishes—

Chris Funkhouser

David to Allen 9 13 88

Allen
Will send you 4 more copies later—you & I alone shared these 2 advance copies
    I hope you're pleased

Dave Cope

w/ Nada Poems

David to Allen 1988 Nov. 21
Cope's "For Billy" poem with subscript: Happy Thanksgiving
    Dave Cope

David to Allen and Bob Rosenthal 1 30 89

616 531 1442

Dear Allen & Bob
Is it possible to send a selection of Allen's recent work (5 or 6 poems) for inclusion in a special issue of *Grand Rapids College Review*, to be published as part of the publicity for Allen's reading here in April? Locals are really gearing up for this thing, as it's been more than 10 years since Allen's read here, & people here are hungry for some real honest poetry.

Please let me know if there's any problems with obtaining poems.

Also, Bob, if you could at the earliest possible opportunity let me know itinerary, so I can make arrangements to pick Allen up etc.

OK—am busy. I read Whitman to eager sophomores last Friday & thought of you.

Paz

Dave Cope

Send poems to me—
I'll get 'em to them.

Right sidebar [in another's hand: sent 2/9/89] in Allen's hand: Vicki or Bob: send xerox of
Sphincter
I went to the movie of life
Spot Anger
Cosmopolitan Greetings
Graphic winces (short form)

See black poetry binder from my drawer
Allen 2/9/89

Attached poems: "Shut The Lights Off," "Sleep," "As The Year Ends," all published in *Fragments from the Stars*. Humana, 1990.

David to Allen 3 28 89

Hi Allen
Thanks for *Song of Napalm* book—I've gotten so many socially conscious books & especially Vietnam vet books in mail recently that I may review them all somewhere.
Enclosed first press release for our April reading—local entertainment magazine; plus variable foot poem I wrote for my kid Will, born 3-16-89. You'll be here exactly one year to the day after I visited you in New York for Brooklyn reading.
Last: Bob should get me, if he can, your reading date in Gaylord, Mi. and address [sidebar: + phone number] where I can reach you there. Unless there are already travel plans for trip from Gaylord to G.R., I'll pick you up there & bring you here. I've taken that whole week off from work; also found you a place to stay here without cats. OK write or call
Hi to Vicky   Thanks again   Dave Cope

Attached poem: "Will," poem reading at bedside after he was born, published in *Fragments from the Stars*. (Humana, 1990).

David to Allen 4 23 89

Hi Allen

This is to say <u>Thanks</u> on behalf of everybody here in G. R. I haven't seen people anywhere excited like that in years: thanks again.

Also, here's some *Press* clippings on the performance. Look above yr article at who was speaking across town the same night—strange humor in editor's placement choices!

Affectionately
(thanks also for quick lesson in Sapphics!)

Dave Cope

Hi to Anne

David to Mary Jo   [unknown correspondent—likely in Allen's office, given last sentence]

Hi Mary Jo   after Allen's and my Apr 20 reading at GVSU, likely late April/early May 1989

I called Pat Bridges + they are in the process of getting tapes of the G. R. reading made up. She says that, barring unforeseen hassles, they should have a copy in mail to Allen within a week.

Holler if you don't get it within 2 weeks.   Dave Cope

David to Allen   12 4 89

Hi Allen

[in Allen's hand with arrow to initial publication request: Write yes, return letter to my box. In office staff's hand: check mark, sent 12/21]

Earlier this fall, I wrote to ask you if I could use "I Went to the Movie of Life" for January issue of *Big Scream*. No answer came back, & as I'll begin on the issue after January first, I'd like to offer you another opportunity to be in the issue. If you have other poems—especially eco-based poems (the issue is mostly Antler-Greg Keeler-Poniewaz eco-poetics)—you'd like published, holler.

As for me, I've been insanely busy this fall—got to teach *Oedipus, The Tempest* & *Othello* for the first time, as well as prose by Hemingway, Stephen Crane & others; also a five week introduction to poetry—I wound up spending most of my time talking about the Provençal tradition & working my way thru Wyatt to Shakespeare sonnets; touched on Whitman & did a freight train class touring thru Williams, Reznikoff, you & Lowell, ending with Ted Berrigan. Other: my 3rd book will be out in January, 119 pages; am really excited about it, as I've not only worked with the usual short objectivist pieces, but also made solid forays into Blakean skull-&-babe-seen-in-the-same-face visions & old music of the spheres organic symphonies, as well as extending the old English alliterative line that has always been my rhythmic home base. I hope you're happy with it as well, & will send copies as soon as it's out.

Other—am hard at work designing a multi-cultural class (American authors of non-white backgrounds) for local J. C. So far have chosen Dudley Randall's fine anthology *The Black Poets*, M. L. King's *Why We Can't Wait*; & am looking at possibly using Frank Chin's collection of stories from North Point, a multi-cultural anthology out of U. of Georgia that Antler got in, *An Ear to the Ground,* & have Bertha Sanchez Bello working on translating Martí's *Nuestra America* for it as well.

Silberman called Rakosi & says he's alright after earthquake. I heard you & Philip Glass were here after it happened. All my boys are hollering they can't wait for next summer in Boulder, & neither can I. Write soon & let me know which poems I should use for *Big Scream*.

Dave

PS I'll enclose cover mock-up for my new *Fragments* w. this. Cover by Funkhouser (Longs Peak)

Attachment: xerox of proof copy of "Farewell" and of front cover photo for new book, me resting on a slope on Longs Peak, with separate page showing lettering to be superimposed over photo for final cover.

Steven Taylor and Allen at breakfast, Marine Street Apartments, 1980s.
Photo by Christopher Funkhouser.

Cover for coursepack ed. David Cope for his three sessions at Beats and Other Rebel Angels Conference. Photo by Darlene Kazmarczyk, Grand Rapids Community College, 1993. Coursepack pub. 1994.

Anne Waldman, cover of *Big Scream* 47. Photo by Kai Sibley.

Jim Cohn, 4th of July trail to Continental Divide, 1994.
Photo by David Cope

1990-1996: Young Poets for Scream, Beats & Other Rebel Angels, Spring Readings for Gelek Rinpoche

David Cope backstage at Hill Auditorium, Ann Arbor, Mi. 1995. Photo by Allen Ginsberg.

Prelude

After 1990, my written correspondence with Allen was more rare, and—the lessons learned & my turn to pass them on having come, both of us too busy—we communicated more on the telephone and meeting each other at events and retreats. Other than one letter and one script responding to his office staff re my letter, Allen's letters to me from this period have not been preserved either in his papers at Stanford or mine at Michigan, though some of my letters suggest that he sent me the manuscripts of younger poets he happened on, or corresponded with me about other matters. Some of them may have been deposited in the manuscripts and correspondence for the annual *Big Screams* that I published during this period, all of these filed in my papers at Michigan, but I haven't had time to check that out. We met at his readings or workings together at Naropa, and during his retreat with the Jewel Heart Community —sitting quietly together for an hour, as after his landmark reading of "Kaddish" at Ann Arbor Feb. 95, or dinner with Allen & Steve Silberman in Boulder café, Summer 94. No longer any need on my part to voice enthusiasms & excitements or query for connections, nor on Allen's part to promote my work & drive himself crazy doing it: now the pleasure was mainly sitting together and sharing time. There are letters I sent him during the 1995-1996, gathered in my unpublished selected letters; these were not in the Stanford pdfs, but I've included them here.

David to Allen Two dates: 3-22-90 in my hand; 4/10 in, I think, Allen's.

Hi Allen

I send this second copy of my *Fragments* as Library edition. Hope you enjoyed the first. View out your 12th st. window in March 88 is on p. 66. Other poems from my visit to you then are on pages 40, 41, and 73.

Busy here. Jim Cohn has practically written another book—turning out 5 or 6 really fine poems almost every week. Strange dialogue with Jeff Poniewaz, who seems to think my insistence on particulars is an attack on his and Antler's work. God save me from such arguments. Ruggia's in despair, divorced & racing from country to country writing travelogues; I can't seem to reach him. Joel K's reading *Aeneid* in Latin.

Too much mail now; I managed to set up a multi-cultural class (Afro-Am, Caribbean, Chicano, Native American + Asian-Am. Literature) for J. C.; reading Ida B. Wells' *Autobiography, Tempest*, & other Shakespeare plays. (I teach *The Tempest* in one of my classes). I think of you often.

Peace Dave Cope

Allen to David Cope's annotation: 4/2/90

Dear David—
Got your new book, thanks, excellent
These poems were in a sheaf handed to me in a theater in L.A.—
kind of nice—can return to sender if you don't want the clutter—As ever

Allen

Been seeing Czech "Plastic People" associates here—going to Prague April 25—May 5 with Sakaki Nanao

Allen Ginsberg

David to Bob Rosenthal 7 14 90

Hi Bob
Could you or Allen send me a CD copy of *The Lion for Real*? Charge me your going prices—I couldn't afford it when reading took place at Naropa, but am home now & better able.

Conference was an interesting & enjoyable experience; working with Gary Snyder & Peter Warshall & Bill DeVall was a real pleasure. Allen, Anne & Don's performance was highlight of the week; Ed Sanders as well. I climbed Mt. Audubon with Antler (13,200 ft) & met lots of young kids & also middle-aged good poets, too. Would've enjoyed having tea with you at 8 a.m. as we did in 1980.

OK, that's all.
Dave Cope

David to Allen 8 27 90

Hi Allen
I xeroxed a good portion of the enclosed ms., which I am sending back as per Jackie's note. Have also received another ms. from Richard Cole, & will publish some of these poems in new *Big Scream* due out Jan. 1991. I think this guy has an unusually pure strain of Reznikoff-style objectivism going, & he's charming, too. Will send some of these to Jim Cohn at *Napalm Health Spa*, some to Funk & some to Joel Kuszai at *Big Fireproof Box*.

As for me, have completed & revised my *Early Poems 1971-1982*, which contains many of the earlier works that you encouraged me for, e.g. "The Museum of Meat." Also have written & completed a prose book *The Blue Notebook*, which contains essays on everything from the sonnet from 1292-1610 to Rested poetics & eco essays to autobiographical shots with early teenage piss in the mouth orgy memories & family memories as well. Lanigan has both of these now. & am working on my next book; designed a multi-cultural course for J. C. featuring Tibetan Buddhist & Vietnamese Buddhist writings, M. L. King, Lorca, Neruda & later Hispanic American writers, Langston Hughes & Robert Hayden, plus later authors, Native American writings from *Shaking the Pumpkin* and *Beyond the Trail of Broken Treaties*, historical retrospective of Native American battles for liberty, with special consideration for legal maneuverings. Am also carrying on battle with my senator thru the mail, [on his stance] against flagburning, & have circulated our "Declaration of Interdependence" to various senators & congressmen. Put a new roof on my garage, reshingled it & am now painting peaks; & am in the heaviest part of the canning season—blueberry jam on Friday, pickles, sauerkraut & so far two big batches of my own homemade spaghetti sauce. Went to a ballgame & saw Cecil Fielder sock one right out of Tiger stadium.

As for this Richard Cole, I believe he should be seeking a publisher; perhaps if you wrote Lanigan (Humana Press, Crescent Manor, P. O. Box 2148, Clifton, New Jersey 07015) with personal message, he might look it over.

Finally I wrote earlier & asked for CD of *The Lion for Real*. Send me one & bill me.

OK, All for now. Again I enjoyed working with you this past summer & look forward to future times together at Naropa.
      Hi to Jackie.

        Peace
        Dave Cope

P.S. Will send my books to Richard Cole—*Fragments* and Nada Anthology.

David to Allen   11 13 90

Hi Allen

 I thought you'd find the enclosed poem interesting, & send it along with prayer for peace & wishes for you to have happy Thanksgiving.

 Big Scream will be out within 1 ½ months—including several poets you sent me.

 Have applied to teach full-time & quit janitor job next fall. If hired, I'll teach 2-3 courses of freshman comp, a multicultural literature course I designed myself, a yearlong "Survey of British lit"—beginning with *Beowulf* & going strait thru to Seamus Heaney, and either an "Introduction to Philosophy" (survey of major philosophers from Plato to Russell & Wittgenstein) or "Intro to Ethics."

 Chris Ide has called me several times. I missed your Michigan readings in Oct—I was reading in Canton NY & spent time with Jim Cohn in high peaks wilderness of Adirondacks.

        Peace
        Dave Cope

Attachment: Early draft of "[In] Fitful Sleep"—vehement satire, dream of war between US led coalition and Iraq, which would not formally begin until 17 January 1991.

David to Allen   December 17, 1991

Dear Allen (& Jacqueline—thanks for sending these)

Thank-you for thinking of *Big Scream* for Greg Winters' "Eleven Poetry Shorts," which I'll of course publish in this January issue—story thru accompanying letters particularly sad & moving, a boy excited with you as new friend, on fire with poesy & apparently well loved by his girlfriend, cut off in his beginning.

Funny, I'd been thinking of you—I taught *Howl & Other Poems* in 4 hour multicultural literature class the other night, introducing you via videotape of yr reading with me at Grand Valley in 1989. "Howl" sparked intense discussion in class over problems of coming out, scorn from homophobes + dignity of one's experience, & how one deals with minds set in hatred, immovable.

I don't know if I told you about my "change of life"—resigned janitor job + am now teaching full time (19 hours of classes) plus going to grad school at WMU (my first class was on Marlowe-Shakespeare-Jonson—I did papers on *Comedy of Errors* & anti-semitism in medieval & renaissance texts, focusing on *Merchant of Venice* + *The Jew of Malta*; next class is on Dante). Am also 2/3 thru my next book, *Coming Home*—Jim Cohn has a copy of current ms.—you want one? Funkhouser will publish chapbook of my new work in Feb—10 pages or so. New *Big Scream* will be out in January—poems by Antler (lovely multi-sexual rhapsodies!), Andy Clausen, Jim + others—of course I'll send—

> OK Peace & Many Fine Poems come to you
> in the coming year! with affection & respect
> Dave Cope

Attachment: "The River," poem.

David to Allen 2 5 92

Hi Allen
News that you're feeling better couldn't suit me better.

As per your earlier request, I sent two copies of *Big Scream* to Greg Winters' girlfriend. Also, I'll publish one or two of Jim Ferguson's poems you just sent— "Park Slope" is a good candidate.

Finally, I would love to see some of your own new poems & publish those, if you're up for sending out a manuscript.

Busy here, teaching, writing, taking classes in Dante & in post-structural criticism. I'll get my masters in medieval & renaissance poesy with concentration on Shakespeare. Taught Whitman & Reznikoff in my classes last week—Reznikoff's "Depression" gives them plenty of room to think about the historicity of homelessness.

Thanks again.

> Dave Cope

Typed on lower part of page: "The Sleepers," poem published in *Coming Home*. Humana, 1993.

David to Allen   4 24 92

Hi Allen

Haven't written for a long time—I just had a lovely weekend with Anne + Jim (see poster) + wanted to share the pleasure with you. We taught my students, gave 3 readings + raised over $200 for AIDs Resource Ctr. local.

I'm publishing the "LEIR," section of Anne's *De Iovis* in next *Big Scream*. Have you got any new poems esp. objectivist mode (but whatever you'd like to send!) to send me? Next *Big Scream* is Jan. 93.

All reports here say your health is better—I've dreamed on it & pray you're well.

I remember when we both slept 20 hours in your apartment—both of us exhausted from pushing too hard; we woke in time to do work at Brooklyn College. I still correspond with Peter Money, who has evolved into quite a poet + editor.

Hello + Peace to Peter Orlovsky too.

        Love
        Dave Cope

David to Allen   6 28 92

Hi Allen

The enclosed suite of poems my newest batch—I hope you enjoy them. I wrote Bob Rosenthal to set up your possible visit here in Feb 93—but wanted to get in closer poetical contact, too, hence this letter.

Am having a strange summer, my first since quitting janitor job, where I can wander in fields & neighborhoods all day dreaming, or take bus downtown + noodle in libraries. Jim Cohn's heartbroken again—his father never showed up at their planned meeting in San Diego after 30 year absence. I think he's handling it OK—many friends to the rescue, quiet moments at Boulder Creek with his brother.

I'm teaching 4 nights a week (3 hr. each—2 ½ weeks poesy, 1 week short stories, 2 ½ weeks Sophocles' *Oedipus Rex* + Shakespeare *Othello*. Am researching political uses to which Shakespeare's *Richard II, Henry V, Julius Caesar* + *Coriolanus* have been put—weird censorship stories + history of amputation, Orson Welles' Mussolini + Hitler *Coriolanus*, Essex rebellion against Elizabeth, etc.

Write soon; I miss you—send poems if you got 'em. How's Peter? Strange breakdown stories reach my ear—he was good to me in 1980.

        Peace Dave Cope

Attachments: "The Abandoned City," "Satie & Dante," "Each Wound Became a Voodoo Mouth," "El Mozote," "The Lovers Sleep," "Weeks on End, Work & Worry—," "Out of the Ruins," most freeform unrhymed "weird sonnets"—all except "Weeks on End, Work & Worry" published in *Coming Home*. Humana, 1993.

David to Allen Labor Day 92

Hi Allen

Humana is publishing my 4th book, *Coming Home,* next spring, & I thought I'd send you a copy of the ms. for your bedtime reading. I'm busy as ever—Bob Rosenthal should contact me as soon as he has time, re your reading here in G.R. next Feb or March. G.R.C.C. administrators were receptive to the visit as long as I don't spend more than I did for Anne and Jim's visit last Spring. We'll videotape & take still photos too. Other: Chris Ide stopped in to see me after his recent fall off the wagon; he's as well as might be expected, working on poems & preparing to spend the winter in a halfway house up in Sault Saint Marie. Address after Sept: New Hope, 1139 E. Portage, Sault Ste. Marie, Mi. 49783. LONG winter up there.

Also, Jim Cohn has settled in with his brother in Louisville CO—once he finds a job, I think he'll be OK. He's got an entire book of top-drawer stuff plus his Disabilities Anthology, & is stumping for a publisher. Otherwise, lotsa shit in the mail.

I'm teaching 19 hours this semester—including Multicultural lit. class that again will end with your "Howl." One student returned here from Alaska or some other faroff place to sign up for the class, on your recommendation. Also doing an independent study—2 essays, one on performance history of *Julius Caesar* & the other on women characters in *As You Like It, Much Ado, & Measure for Measure*. Did a study this summer of Marlowe's *Hero & Leander,* translated Musaeus' 5th cy. version of the poem into English, & analyzed epyllia such as the *Hylas* of Theocritus & Catullus 64: *The Marriage of Peleus & Thetis*. So I've been busy with a lot of tradition work, not simply academic if it informs my poesy. Close to the nose! I hope you're well—write soon, if you get time.

David to Allen 28 Dec 92

Superscript note in, I think, Allen's hand: Bob FYI

Hi Allen

First, thanks for sending Richard Nager + Jim Ferguson works. I'm publishing Ferguson's work in current *Big Scream*, due out before end of January (issue features Anne W's "Leir," a piece I fell in love with when she read here last spring). Lotsa great new mss. in the mail—booklength stuff by Robert Borden, Bruce Hayes, Mike Pingarron + Richard Wilmarth—Wilmarth's book-elegy for his mother a moving journey through moments leading towards her death, in some ways like Reznikoff's "Kaddish."

Have you seen Jimmy Cohn's research on Pound's St. Elizabeth years? Wish I had a million bucks so I could publish all these guys!

Re your reading here—I have 7/8 of the funding I'll need to pull it off, & my boss is working on getting the rest. I've rented a fine old medieval-style church for the reading.

More later—happy new year!

Peace
Dave

David to Allen 1 16 93

Hi Allen

I'm pleased you enjoyed the magazine—Kevin Bezner's one of those who appeared in the mailbox—hardly know him—but will get to—

Have started publicity for yr. reading here—college station—TV—announces it every 2 minutes 24 hrs a day—local mags + papers, then to W. Mich. colleges, Lansing, Ann Arbor, Detroit. Teaching 18 hr. a week—they gave me a philosophy course—Intro to Philo—weird to be teaching Plato & Marcus Aurelius, enjoyable—tho I'd rather work with Sappho & Theocritus—maybe in years to come—

Lanigan's publishing my *Coming Home*, 4th book, this spring—

All for now—see you soon

Peace
David

Collaborative Document, David and Allen 2 19-20 93

I wrote descriptions of Allen's two appearances at GRCC and at Fountain Street Church on February 19, 1993, and before he left for his next gig, gave him the typed copy for edit; he made edits as he felt were proper, and I made the proper changes, later publishing this in my course book for my creative writing classes, *A Poet's Sourcebook*:

Poetry at GRCC: Allen Ginsberg:
February 19, 1993

ATC Lectures: 1:00-3:00

Allen spoke to a packed auditorium, mostly students and professors, but with a few press reporters and local poets. In the first hour, Allen chanted the "Prajna Paramita Sutra" and spoke about his political concerns, reading from his "New Democracy Wish List" (publ. *New York Newsday*, 1-20- 93); he stated that "hyper-rationalization, hyper-industrialization & hyper-technology create chaos," citing military industrial complexes, worldwide pollution, command economies that place profit before the planet's real needs as examples of the principle. He also focused on his concerns about censorship and claimed that only the freedom to say what one thinks will restore sanity to governments and societies across the globe; citing J. Edgar Hoover as an example, he showed how the fear of revealing one's true self can distort national priorities and create a complex web of denial in which crime and homophobic behavior flourish.

Allen also spoke about political correctness, questioning the audience about the problem of allowing free speech when that free speech involves hatred of gays and minorities; his position is that governments should "punish deeds, not words." He later responded to questions about writing and revision, stating the following principles: (1) "lean towards tolerance of your first drafts," depending on them while at the same time revising to eliminate abstraction and to substitute detail. (2) focus your awareness as Kerouac did, by constantly working in the details of the scene and situation; as a result of Kerouac's practice, "everything [comes] from the heart." Finally, he answered a question about arts subsidies, saying that he believes in "democratic appreciation of the arts, even if less-than-great poets get the subsidies." He also posed a question: if one should eliminate subsidies for arts, shouldn't one also eliminate subsidies for Marine Corps marching bands? Finally, he reminded the audience that "normal western developed nations spend much more on the arts than we do. . . there is nothing wrong with government arts subsidies."

In the second hour, Allen answered many questions about writing and about his Buddhist religious practice. First, he pointed out the usefulness of one's dreams as providing materials for one's art, saying that he writes out dreams he remembers, and that those that seem to tell complete stories often can be transcribed directly as poems. To a question regarding the relationship of poetry to music, he claimed that the bond between the two arts goes back to the beginnings of the forms—citing the 12,000 year old Australian Aborigine practice, Homer, Greek choruses that sang and danced, African practices, and such modern forms as African American blues and poet composers such as Bob Dylan and the Beatles. Allen pointed out that even in spoken form, words have a musicality in their sounds. A good poet will be conscious of pitch, and "vocalization is an essential attribute of the poem."

He next answered questions about fundamentalist Christianity and balancing the literary canon. Allen first separated fundamentalists into two groups— "libertarian fundamentalists" and a group he labelled "Stalinists" who "have tried to deny me my fundamental rights to speak my mind." He pointed out that this second group, which includes the likes of Senator Jesse Helms, presents an agenda using language remarkably similar to the language used by Nazis, Stalinists and Maoists in that all four have attempted to "impose their absolutist views on others" and censor freedom of expression by claiming that those works they disagree with are examples of "spiritual corruption" practiced by "degenerate individualists." To the question of balancing the literary canon, Allen responded by naming numerous texts that should be included in teaching literature; among these, he named "The Heart Sutra" the Hindu *Bhagavad Gita* and *Ramayana*, the poems and biography of Milarepa (the Tibetan saint), Lao-Tze, the work of Kabir, African trickster tales and Native American coyote tales, the Australian Aborigine epic, and others, including the earliest written epic, *Gilgamesh*.

Finally, a student asked him if he saw a conflict between the western "extroverted" mindset and the "introverted" eastern mindset in his Buddhist practice. Allen first pointed out that Buddhist practice was not a turning inward or denial of the outer reality, explaining that meditation quiets the mind and allows one to increase sensory appreciation. The point is to increase one's awareness in order to return to the world and help alleviate the suffering that is everywhere. He gave the audience basic instructions on sitting posture ("spine straight, eyes open—neither overly focused nor unfocused; pay attention to the breath exhaling; accept the fact that you cannot concentrate exclusively on that, and sometimes will wander into your thoughts—return to attentiveness to the breath when you become aware"); after this, the poet and entire audience sat silently for three minutes together.

Allen ended the second hour with descriptions of the "ground"—mental attentiveness and tuning—necessary for the process of writing. Quoting Chogyam Trungpa Rinpoche, he said that the first thought that comes into one's mind is the place to start, and stated that one should develop a looseness and acceptance of "one thought following another without hyperlogical or artificially linear progression." Allen cited Keats' idea of "negative capability"—acceptance of contradictions and negations as being necessary to containing a whole vision; he quoted Creeley's idea that "form is never more than an extension of content," and explored Wordsworth's "spots of time"—moments of vividness located in ordinary experience but raised to epiphany by attentiveness to details.

David to Allen in Allen's hand: 6 March '93

Hi Allen
Enclosed is the final report to GRCC administration with tally on page four. I am hoping that with this amount of money, I can go back to administration next year for matching funds & bring several poets in next year—but that's a way off yet. Main concern is: thanks for coming out here. As always, I enjoyed being with you, and learned a whole lot of things as you put poetry in the public's eye.

I'll be in touch. Please let me know if the tapes etc. don't arrive properly. Craig Stutzky says he sent you photos & videotapes, & will get audio later. Hello to Bob & Jacqueline.

Peace

David

David to Allen 25 May 93

Hi Allen
     Thanks for *Pinched Nerves* Eve Packer poems—I've published Ken DiMaggio before—seem to recall you first turned me on to him. Also thanks for "American Sentence" in yr letter—I'll publish with others in next *Big Scream*, which also has some excellent new work by Andy Clausen + Antler.

     Quiet spring here so far—my book still not published—I'll send a copy when it's out. Planting flowers, wandering in my garden watching bees + marveling over new leaves—twice a week I'm taking grad class—Chaucer.
                      Love
                      David Cope

PS Please check proof—
        [in Allen's hand: 4 (illegible) Sent proofs 6/1/93 AG]

David to Allen   28 June 1993
        [in Allen's hand: proofs OK 6/4/93 AG]

Hi Allen + Jacqueline

    Address I have for Ken DiMaggio is the same one you sent the card to—probably no sense in me forwarding it to same address, so I'll send it back to you—Have you published the "American Sentence" on the postcard? If not, may I include it with the other "American Sentences" I have for next *Big Scream*? [left sidebar in Allen's hand: illegible] If so, please advise how to space on the page. I'll send copy w. this.

Also enclosed, booklet from my 2 hour reading + discussion— "Eard-Stapa," Chaucer, Dante, Whitman—thought you'd enjoy it.

I'm busy—my new *Coming Home* book looks to be published in August now—a series of delays have held it up. Spent 6 weeks in graduate Chaucer class—"Parliament of Fowls," *Troilus + Criseyde*, the best of the *Canterbury Tales*—pleasurable way to spend springtime + early summer. Am now reading + outlining all of Shakespeare's tragedies for fall class + my own pleasure. I start teaching again in July—off to Maryland these next 5 days, to Freer Gallery + musing in hills beyond Wash. DC.

        Love
        Dave Cope

Attachment: "Old Man" poem later published in *Silences for Love* **(Humana, 1998).**

David to Allen 28 July 1993

Hi Allen

 I'm enclosing preliminary draft copy of *Sourcebook* for Multicultural Lit. class I teach—which has your "Old Love Story" and "I Love Old Whitman So" on pages 109-111. There are 2 typos, which I'll fix when we go to print—probably not this semester—the college has put the course on hold because of funding shortage. Anyroad, this draft copy is current state of my researches re multicultural literature, & I thought you might enjoy a copy.

 I'm busy as usual, somewhat isolated here in Michigan—tho I did visit Gettysburg battlefield + Holocaust Museum in Wash DC for a week. My gardens are full of flowers. I've taken up walking, eliminated coffee + tea from diet as per yr recommendation when you were here last Feb.—ulcer's disappeared. My *Coming Home* book still not published—Lanigan says it should be out in August—

 I'll send you a copy then.

  Other—great blues tape in mail from Andy Clausen—have you heard this most recent?
      OK all for now—

      Love
      Dave Cope

David to Allen In Allen's hand: 8/4/39 [93]

[Superscript: Find so I can recycle intro to his book (illegible) recommendations—Allen]

Dear Allen

 I'll be finishing my master's degree at Western Michigan University this coming spring, and am thinking of going on to get a PhD, probably either in medieval or renaissance English poetry, in poetry writing or in multicultural literature. If you could have time, could you write me a recommendation for entry into this program?

 So far, I don't think academic writing has adversely affected my poems, & if I get an advanced degree, it'll help me establish a larger forum for poets who might not otherwise get a hearing.

 OK, all for now.

Peace
David

      [right sidebar below, in office staff's hand:
      Is this too late? *Quiet Lives* intro attached]

David to Allen undated, likely Jan 1994

[Superscript in another hand: To: Jewel Heart 313 434 6770, and below my drawing of lips, my phone number, 616-531-1442]

Hi Allen

Just a note to say I hope I can spend a few moments with you in Ann Arbor Feb 4—barring hellfire + ice storms, I'll be there.

Also—you're reading in Hill Auditorium almost 25 years after your 1969 November pro-peace Moratorium reading there [note: October 12], when *Planet News* was new, & I, a young poet full of unresolved rage first heard you read "Howl" & broke down in tears—

A lot of miles behind us since. I'm well—hi to Bob & Jacqueline—

See you soon

Love
Dave Cope

Left sidebar: PS Have arranged for Antler + Jeff to read at GRCC in March, using monies raised by yr reading here last year.

David to Allen 2 5 94

Hi Allen

<u>Superb</u> reading last night in Ann Arbor esp. "Father Death"—most moving performance of those I've heard—also new poem that begins in yr apartment + goes down to Christine's—you outdid yourself all night, tho.

I <u>am</u> worried about that cough you have, tho. Take care of your voice—drink <u>lots</u> of water.

OK, all for now—see you maybe in April (sorry we didn't connect—the crowds—but I had no real expectations anyways. Good just to be anonymous in crowd, too.

Love
Dave Cope

PS. Antler + Jeff're coming to GRCC next month for ecopoetical colloquium. Program structured like yours here last year, but they'll also do 2 hours of Whitman, for which I can't wait—

David to Allen Undated, likely late Feb-early Mars 94

Hi Allen

Enclosed poster features yr photo of Antler—thought you'd like a copy.

I've already sent for my tickets to Dalai Lama's 1:00 pm talk on April 23 (Ann Arbor)—any chance I could sit with you then?

Hope you've gotten a chance to get some rest. I've got a week off now—hiking local trails, catching up with friends, loafing.

109

Peace
David Cope

[in Allen's hand: Ans'd p.c. 3/14/94]

Attached poems, "Sarajevo Market Massacre" and "February 25, 1944," both later published in *Silences for Love* **(Humana, 1998). Also photocopy of Antler & Jeff Poniewaz reading poster, with Allen's handwritten emendations (sent back one day before reading, thus I was unable to make changes in time).**

David to Allen   10 April 1994

Hi Allen

Could you send me a copy of yr poem re New York City parade after the Gulf War? [right sidebar with line to note, likely in office staff's hand: I already sent After the Big Parade 4/14/94]

I'm working on a little anthology to use for my classes this summer, & I need recent example of political-prophetic strain in yr work. See enclosed Contents page to see how it'll fit.

Also, I should ask yr permission to print the others in course sourcebook I'll print for the class. Hope I can see you Apr. 23 at Dalai Lama speech—if not, we'll cross this summer. Antler & I had a ball together—tho too little time—this spring.

Peace
David

PS Any suggestions to add to my list? Will also have *Big Scream* type cover w. sideview photo from yr. visit here last year.

I can't wait to see you & share time

                                          [right sidebar in Allen's hand: OK AG
                                           Did you send poem? It's attached AG]

Note in Allen's hand to his office staff   Addendum to Form Letter as of 5/23/94.

     What's further remarkable is that Mr. Cope is an excellent scholar with a wide range of earnest interests in prosody, form + poetic lineage beyond his own century, as well as outside of European culture. I hope he'll be enabled to polish his learning with studies for advanced degrees in universities.

                                                   A Ginsberg.
                                                        with credentials

                    Use original blurb + this

Sent 5/23/94
File Dave Cope

David to Allen 1 June 94

Dear Allen

Thanks for your notices recommending me for PhD program; as it turned out, I used the introduction to *Quiet Lives* and was accepted in May. Will concentrate on medieval poetics and Shakespeare's era (I did most of my masters work on Shakespeare, Dante + Chaucer and their contemporaries). So, thanks.

Other. I'm enclosing proof copy of sourcebook I edited for my 3 classes at Naropa in July.

Hope it meets with your approval (line from this sentence to bottom of page: cover photo will reproduce better on printer's machines]. Will also distribute copies of *Big Scream* 31 to them so they'll be able to pick up on current lineage practice.

OK all for now. See you in July.

Love
David

PS have also enclosed notes from Dalai Lama's talk in Ann Arbor—thought you'd enjoy.

David to Allen 1994 July 21

Hi Allen

Chris's funeral was a wrenching time, though we all worked our way through it. Thanks for your support for Karen Ide + service in Boulder.

Also thanks for giving me a place in your tribute Beats & Rebel Angels—a real privilege for me.

Peace
David Cope

PS. We're working on doing a selected poems for Chris this fall. Could you write a short blurb or introduction for him?

Attached poem "Memory in Love" is one of my two elegies for Chris Ide, both published in *Silences for Love*. (Humana, 1998).

The following letters come from my digital files of my correspondence,
and are gathered in my Selected Letters 1992-2001.
This collection remains unpublished,
but a manuscript copy may be found in The David Cope Papers
at the University of Michigan Special Collections Resource Center.

David to Allen 17 Feb 95

Hi Allen

After our time together last night, I mused on your concern about emotions overcoming the performance of "Kaddish." Your advice to me when I had this problem was to tell me to remember to breathe deeply enough in the pauses between phrases, and not to hurry the performance. (I didn't feel rushed as a listener last night, & recognizing that you had an immense task at hand before coming to fugue, guessed that you could build natural pauses into the long opening, to plan for them at key points in text). Also, would returning to meditation help?

No gripes here in any case—the moments when your emotions rose up did not strike me as self-pity, as you called it, but rather intimated your humanness—that wounds sometimes do move the heart & that even the Kind King can be so touched. I felt privileged to be there.

Do suggest that you work more new materials into the earlier half of the reading—yr version of Amazing Grace a good start.

David to Allen 7 April 96

Hi Allen

As per your warning to send anything else I might want considered for *The Nation* quickly, I'm sending the enclosed—first 2 much newer, the second 2—well, I'm not sure if I sent these before. So here they are.

Yr reading in Ann Arbor—now annual holiday for me: the objectivist piece you opened with, detailing daily habits, brush teeth, take shit, read *Times*, etc. was great pleasure, as was "Kapish" chant, "The Ballad of the Skeletons," & yr homeless version of "Amazing Grace" which spurred a lot of talk & searching thru old wisdom books among theology students I stayed with that night.

The whole reading was fine, but these were the stand-outs. Also, do you have Geoffrey Managh's address? I'll publish him in next issue *Big Scream*. Peter or Bob could send it to me via e-mail if you like: dcope@post.grcc.cc.mi.us

OK, that's it. Peace

Dave Cope, Andy Clausen and James Ruggia. Hoboken, photo by Sharon Guynup.

Ghost in the Machine. Photo by Christopher Funkhouser.

Anne Waldman and Ken Mikolowski in the University of Michigan Residential College library, 2009. Photo by David Cope.

David Cope editing. Photo by Jon Dambacher.

CODA:

The Intense Finale

Sunflowers & Locomotives: Songs for Allen. Nada, Fall 1997. Cover photo of Allen Ginsberg on 12th Street fire escape, by Christopher Funkhouser.

Dave to Jim Cohn 25 May 97

Hi Jim

Just back from 49th day celebration of Allen's life & of closing the bardo. Dunno if I told you, but I had originally decided not to go—too much grief at this point—yet when I sent my contribution for Allen's memory into Jewel Heart, I had included my "for allen" elegy—& Debbie Burr at JH submitted it, without my knowing, in their poetry contest. As fate would have it, I won the contest & was thus one of the featured readers, with lots of free tickets to give to others. Here's a recap:

Susie, Jane, Willie & I arrived in Ann Arbor about noon yesterday, & as we couldn't check into our hotel until 3, we stopped at the Michigan Union (where I had proposed to Sue March 15, 1970) & had lunch, later walking across campus to the Exhibit Museum, passing the spot where John Kennedy first proposed a peace corps in campaign speech 1960; passing the LSA Building, where Sue had been given a concussion by Ann Arbor cops as they threw her and other protesters down the stairs to paddy wagons (Fall 1969, protest for student-run bookstore, one of many protests that fall); past Angell, Mason, & Haven Halls, where I studied under Robert Hayden & first thrilled to Shakespearean goldmine; past the Grad Library where your letters, my letters, Allen's letters, my manuscripts, etc. are stored; across the famed diag—site of so many student-generated actions over the years; and to the museum, where Willie wanted to see dino bones & I was eager to see Native American floor, which features real dugout & birchbark canoes. After wandering thru these halls for some time, I packed the family up at 2:30 & headed them out to hotel, checking in around 2:45 so I could make sound check at Hill Auditorium at 3:00.

Raced downtown & wandered in backdoor: Natalie Merchant had just arrived, & Bob Rosenthal and Peter Hale were standing in doorway. Lovely reunion—Bob, I think, still striving to let go after all those years of closer-connection-than-anybody, handed me his new chapbook & talked of his pride in the festschrift volume he and Bill Morgan had edited for Allen's sixtieth. Now with a beard, he actually looks younger than as I remember him. Peter answered my questions about Gregory (still struggling to adjust, relapse into dope) and Peter Orlovsky, who's handling it well. Peter O, Peter H., and Anne are leaving for Milan today (day after), to see Fernanda Pivano, Allen's Italian translator. We talked at some length, reminiscing not only Allen but Chris Ide (Peter was close to Chris, esp. in Boulder, where they hung out with Steve Miles). I then completed my sound check run-thru of poem, looking out into vast cavernous Hill Auditorium where Allen had read "Howl" to enormous overflow audience in November 1969 [note: October 12], bringing us all to tears, & where he'd performed "Howl" in 1995, "Kaddish". in 1996 [see note re dates] to audiences nearly as large. This May 24 show, too, was scheduled before he got sick—he and Patti were going to again raise money for Gelek. As I finished my sound check, Gelek and the Gyuto monks arrived and sat down to do theirs—he recognizing me immediately from my visits to Allen backstage & from my visit to Gun Lake retreat—big smile, thanking me for coming to be a part. I sensed a tentativeness about him that I hadn't seen before: he and Allen had not only been partners in the enterprise of Jewel Heart, but right from the first time I saw them together I'd noted that they genuinely enjoyed each other's company, like real true spiritual brothers—and this day, I saw Gelek's vulnerability at the loss—it was a beautiful, tender thing, the master's grief, there like a single cloud in a bright sky, yet never clouding his attentiveness. I sat for some time listening to their rehearsal, then realized I should get back to feed Sue & the kids, hotfooting it out just as Patti Smith's musicians pulled into parking lot.

Back at hotel, I took a hot bath, dressed up in my one fancy suit—Anne Waldman later remarked that I looked great in it & that Allen would've appreciated it—& took the family to Bill Knapp's restaurant, where I had broccoli quiche, coffee & milk. We got down to the auditorium at about 6:45, wandering thru the big crowd of old hippies, curious young poets, old professors, etc. to get inside. I'd known that Anne was going to introduce me after her performance, & also knew she'd want to have a little information, so I skedaddled backstage after installing Sue & kids in seats. I also knew coming back to Ann Arbor would have other haunted associations for Anne—Ted Berrigan & Alice had their first romance during their time here, & coming back here would undoubtedly bring the innocence of those days back to Anne—so I asked her about it. Her face clouded briefly & then she brightened, "yes, this is where they fell in love"—pleased, I think, that I would remember that with her. Just before the show started, I walked out on stage to make sure my friend Phil Jung & his wife and Carmen & Craig had arrived (I'd gotten them tickets).

OK, the bell went off backstage & the celebration began, audience of 1,400 smaller than earlier performances but still substantial, especially given that the U of M school year was over weeks before & most of the students had already gone home. First, the monks, then local professor representing Rabbi Zalman greeted us & gave numerological & mystical reasons why this date was auspicious for Allen's closing the bardo & for our coming together; he then recited the kaddish. The first portion of the program ended with "Amazing Grace" sung in soaring cadences by a young woman who must have blast furnaces for lungs. Intermission.

Poets came next: Anne read first & I really wish I'd had her script to follow—she was working tornadoes of syllables, poem rising & rising to crescendo, never letting us off the hook, I've never seen her more commanding, more on fire—& the audience jumped right with her. Then she introduced me, saying Allen would be pleased that I'd won contest (Bob & Peter & I backstage enjoying the irony of a contest being the means to put me up where I belong), calling me "one of Allen's heart sons"—which touched me deeply. I recall hugging her as I stepped into spotlight—delivered the poem relaxed, conversational—finally doing what Allen had told me to do all along ("David, others may need to put on a dramatic show, but your poems are good enough where you should just read 'em—cut the theatrics!") & pleased that he must be out there somewhere pleased that I'd finally learned the lesson. Big applause, & then Bob went out & read Allen's last poems—same quirky humor & finesse phrasing in longer piece, & his last poem "Gone, Gone, Gone" like a blues mantra, stately, Bob reading so perfectly you could imagine Allen's voice not so differently. After Bob, Natalie Merchant did several songs at grand piano—nice girl, very pretty with black hair & sparkling eyes, a bit shy among big mouth poets; then Allen's musician friends (Detroit & Toledo classical musicians who'd accompanied him every time he came to this area) did "Father Death"—eerie violin taking lead where Allen's voice would've been before. Finally, Patti Smith and her band came out & concluded the evening with her reading of her own elegy for Allen, Hank Williams' "I'm So Lonesome I Could Cry," Dylan's "Wicked Messenger," & Patti's own tune & arrangement of the "Footnote to Howl," which brought the house down. Finally, there was giant video of Allen doing "Meditation Rock" two years before at Hill: "learn a little patience and generosity—generosity, generosity, generosity, and GENEROSITY!"

Crowd dispersed, & Bob, Peter, Anne, Sue & I, Carmen & Craig, Ken Mikolowski & others all met at the Red Hawk bar (Craig took Jane & Willie—who were seeing their daddy read for the first time & had cheered me on—over to his place, where Carmen's brother Caitlin treated them to videos & movies while we partied & had reunions), where we all yakked & ate & drank til about 1 am, Sue doing a version of "Rock & Roll Nigger" that had Anne in stitches. Sue herself had cried for Chris Ide during the celebration—she'd been unable to when he died, I think because she had loved him & was pissed at how many lives he'd fucked up & how much he'd thrown away; tonight, she saw her ability to find her tears for Chris as Allen's last gift to her. For me, it was so good to see Bob & Anne—a real healing for me—as I told them, it had been hard to stretch across 1000 miles to share grief with everyone else via phone & e-mail & letters, not like hugging & yakking & looking into each other's eyes: I think physical presence is absolute necessity for truly sharing & working out grief—touch & eyes & voiced words convey love like no other medium, O the poem's wild & gentle waves in shared air. Sharing the stage was a special blessing, as was being able to spend time with Peter Hale.

So we came home to hotel late that night, fell asleep, woke up to rainy morning where the kids splashed in indoor hotel pool an hour & I worked out on treadmill among sweating buns of high-powered executives panting with weights & humping machines before we headed out, home to Grandville, relieved, & with a whole new batch of tender memories. So good to see old friends, so good to share voices, so good to be able to do this for Allen, so good to once again see the wide pattern of associations he evoked and continues to evoke in us all. I send this as record of the event: hope you heard me calling—you were here as best as I could keep you through it all.

David to Jim Cohn Excerpt from letter of 19 July 1998

Notes for colloquium (what to recall about "Allen as teacher") (I did not use any of these; in the end, I read my "for allen" and gave away copies of *Sunflowers & Locomotives*, telling how Allen promoted my work, taught me—with Bob Rosenthal—how to do literary contract, criticized my readings & taught me how to tie tie. Yet the notes themselves have some value, so I've included them here. Through the whole week, I did a lot of talking about Allen & the effects of his death on the poetry community. Every personal conversation had that element, as I wanted to have some gauge of what the loss means at this point):

A. ALLEN'S THEMES

1. As Ed Sanders once emphasized, "seek out the best minds" of your generation and develop a supportive network—CONTACT, as William Carlos Williams suggested.
2. Refusal to settle for one dominant approach to poems: endless experimentation with formal qualities of poems and with coding of language.
3. Honesty with the mind's actual thought forms—sexual, political, personal—connected to openness and compassion for others and for oneself.
4. Responsibility to research positions, to hold them responsibly and be able to defend them with integrity.
5. Awareness of lineages—political, spiritual, political—and finding the intersections of these lineages.
6. Continuous effort to break down censorship and to promote freedom of speech.

B. ALLEN AS STUDENT
1. From Whitman: long line, clear eye, openness, sexual freedom, honesty.
2. from Pound: juxtaposition as principle of poetic composition, responsibility to care for and promote the careers of others.
3. from Williams: example of continuous experimentation with lines and modes of expression.
4. from Charles Reznikoff: insistence on close observation of particulars based in everyday experience.

C. ANECDOTAL
5. Reznikoff's memory of Allen carrying his bags for him across Central Park. (from 1973 National Poetry Festival, Allendale, Mi.) In my life:
    a. He gave me an emotional model by which to understand & work on my rages— "Howl" gave me a space to explore my feelings about myself & others at a critical time in my teenage years. Later, he personally advised me that I would never be free until I forgave my father & made peace.
    b. Allen brought me Andy, Jim, James Ruggia, Antler, and through them I met others of my generation, even younger poets like Chris Ide & Chris Funkhouser, connections that have defined my life as a poet, as one of a great crowd of kindred spirits musing through time.
    c. He always severely criticized my performances onstage, always with an eye to improving them. (See my performance caveats, later in this letter—these're lessons I learned the hard way).
    d. He wrote introductions and pushed my work tirelessly for nine years.

  e. Late night at his apartment, he and Steve Taylor turned us all on to Campion and Dowland via singing parts and improvising on the spot.
  f. When I taught Reznikoff at Naropa in 1980, Allen brought me Marsden Hartley's poems.
  g. When I introduced him at GRCC in 1993, Allen taught me how to tie my tie correctly, so it wouldn't flop as much when I leaned over.

D. BUILDING COMMUNITY (LESSONS)

1. to learn how to love each other, in the sense of the journey we make together, the need to recognize that none of us is beyond reproach & that all of us should learn how to forgive each other & not allow idiosyncrasies or anger to affect the long relationship.
2. to treasure each other's works & help get them out to others, to learn how to make connections with others on the same search.
3. to give each other honest criticism without getting stupidly offended.
4. to have fun together, as with the Campion/Dowland story above.
5. to share the deepest emotions & life stories together—to know each other, learning the arcs & lineage of each friend and to appreciate that where we are, where we were, what we want for ourselves are all important.

. . . .

Ed Sanders' Talk on Allen [my notes included with July 19, 1998 letter to Jim Cohn]
July 7, 10:00 am—me just arrived in Boulder

a. Antecedents: repression of Jews in Moscow, underground politics, Decembrist movement.
a. 1903 Bolsheviks formed in London
b. 1905 Bloody Sunday: march on the Winter Palace—many shot dead, which triggered strikes across Russia & a wave of pogroms (pogrom=devastation).
b. Louie's family came to Newark out of this matrix, about 1880s (he was born in US). His family came from the social democrat tradition—they were socialists, pragmatic, more willing to compromise than later Bolsheviks.
c. Naomi's family moved to NYC to escape pogroms in 1905; Mendel Levergunt, her father, became Morris Levy at Ellis Island. Four kids: Eleanor, Naomi, Max, Sam. The family was more aligned with the new communist tradition. Naomi grew up speaking Yiddish, played the mandolin.
d. Naomi's family went to Orchard St. in NYC; Morris opened a candy store, later moved to Newark. As a teenager, Naomi had her first breakdown, in which light was painful to her eyes—she was kept in the dark for three weeks. Later, there would be some tension in the Ginsberg family over Naomi, though photos of Louie with her show great hope and love.

e. Louie and Naomi: their son Eugene was named after Gene Debs (socialism won over communism). At Camp Nishkidigot (spelling uncertain) near Woodstock, Allen learned his first songs.
f. Allen was born in 1926, and Naomi was in sanitarium in 1929 after pancreas surgery. Allen's concern for family perhaps grows from the intense determination to keep family together, not exclude his mother. In 1930, Naomi returned to the family in Paterson.
g. In 1935, Naomi experienced another depression related to light, and went to Greystone for shock treatments. Her paranoia grew, connected perhaps to Great Depression and the rise of fascism and Nazism in Europe. Meanwhile, Allen was growing up and slowly discovering he was gay, amassed files on Spanish Civil War, Nazis, etc., clipping news stories like "Jack the Clipper."
h. There were fierce debates over politics in Allen's family. The Moscow show trials, isolation of Trotsky, etc. threw leftists in USA into confusion.
i. By the end of high school, Allen knew he was gay, and wanted to go to Columbia, perhaps to become a labor lawyer. Naomi was hospitalized again. In 1943, Allen took a vow (he was prone to vows even in his poems): if he got into Columbia, he would devote his life to helping the workers—and, Ed says, he did in some sense fulfill that vow, becoming "a labor lawyer without a shingle."
j. Allen enrolled in 1943—an interesting mix of professors including Lionel Trilling and Meyer Shapiro, the marxist art critic. Confused, he met a young republican named Kerouac and William Burroughs in December of 1943.
k. Early on, he was heavily influenced by rhymed poetry, especially the work of Thomas Wyatt, Campion, and Christopher Smart. This early immersion in rhyme paid off during the spontaneous period later, re ease of working sound. He made lists of music, operas to listen to, and Burroughs had a library where Allen first read Baudelaire, etc. Sharing books important to development.
l. What followed was the "bonkers era" of Allen's life; he took a year off and in 1945 worked as welder in the Brooklyn Navy Yard, later fired from Gotham Books. Drafted, he said he was gay, and moved into the Merchant Marine in 1946, just as Jack's dad was dying of cancer. Even during this period, they were talking about the "new vision" that would come later.

The rest of Ed's talk was very familiar to me, so I didn't take notes.

We Four: Christopher Funkhouser, Steven Taylor, Allen, and Chris Ide. Photo by Steve Miles.

Appendix A

Archive Locations, Dating and Placement,
Organization of this Book, and Some Editorial Choices

Original copies of this correspondence are found in The Allen Ginsberg Papers at the Stanford University Special Collections Library, as follows: 1976-1979 (Box 94, folders 1, 2, 3, 4); 1980-1989 (Box 219, folders 62, 63, 64, 65); Box 220, folders, 1,2,3,4, 5, 6, 7); 1990-1994 (Box 321, folders 22, 23, 24). Xerograph copies of these letters and original copies of the Allen Ginsberg letters to David Cope are available in The David Cope Papers at the University of Michigan Special Collections Research Center. Both collections may be located in the two libraries' respective finding aids.

Dating and placement of letters: There are two major problems associated with the placement of my letters to Allen. First, I neglected to date many of my own letters, and second, the dates placed on them by someone in Allen's office are often at odds with the internal evidence of the letters. I worked diligently to remedy this by coordinating internal evidence in my letters via Allen's, thus integrating his with mine. In a few cases, a letter posed a significant problem, as there was no clear internal evidence in my letter to place it in relation to (a) internal evidence in Allen's letters from the same period, and (b) the content or attitudes expressed in my own letters, to which it was connected via placement in the Stanford archive. The problem crops up throughout the files, but a few examples will suffice to illustrate the problem:

<The initial letter in the Stanford pdf, noted at c. 1976 Feb 10, is actually from some time after Allen's letter of January 25, 1977. *Mind Breaths*, subject of my response, was not published until 1977; the ref. to Allen's "American Airlines" letter (here recalled as Pan Am Airlines letter) of January 25, 1977, also dates it in 1977. Because the date of that letter is later than the one ascribed to this one and the subject of this letter includes a youthful response to 1977's *Mind Breaths*, I have placed this letter after the January 25, 1977 letter from Allen.

<My letter misdated to "ca. 1977" (and found far back in the 1976-1979 group) is my response to Allen's March 18, 1976 letter to me, thanking him for his appreciation of my *Stars* chapbook. In my letter, I also asked that he send a copy of the chapbook to Charles Reznikoff. Allen responded to my Reznikoff request in his letter of April 12, 1976, giving me the news that Charles had died recently. I have placed it in its proper place as the second letter in this group.

<Four undated letters were placed at the end of the 1988-1989 Stanford pdf, but per their internal evidence or through internet research clearly came from the following:
        a. the letter placed "likely fall 1980" because of my request for xerox copy of Marsden Hartley's *Selected Poems*, preceding thanks for sending it in 1980 Oct. 20 letter.
        b. the Dec. 1980 letter with my elegy for John Lennon (d. Dec. 8, 1980), the reference to Al Pearlman setting me up with reading in Ann Arbor (Dec. 9, 1980), and the reference to Ken Mikolowski, whom Allen gave his "regards" in his Dec. 30 letter at the end of the year.

    c.   letter of c. January 1981 (via mention of Ferlinghetti giving up the 3-in-1 project and Allen's mention of it in previous January 1981 letter, and mention of my poem "Lelia," which Allen has asked about in that same previous letter—this one answering it).

    d.   the letter dated "likely from 1983 or 1984" (via my correction of evidence in letter to "Seven dead in Buffalo" in my now-lost pamphlet (which itself would likely place it in the heavy period of chapbook publication, 1980-1983, but also via internet story on the 1983 Buffalo propane explosion that killed seven.

Finally, in all cases where I have reassigned a letter to a different position in the sequence, it is due to taking account of contextual evidence in both my letters and Allen's, researching internal references for dates, or in some cases, considering the flow of thought or response in sequence. I do not pretend to have these sequences absolutely correct, as the material is complex, often from as long as 40 years ago, and complicated by my failures to date my correspondence and Allen's staff ascribing dates to letters which are plainly at odds with the evidence within them. Stanford is, of course, not to be faulted in any of this: their sequencing of the letters follows the approximations made by someone in Allen's office who did not consider the internal evidence carefully. In my dating, I am also in the more authoritative position of comparing my letters with Allen's for the first time, and of building the sequence from placing the letters together in one collection.

Organization

I have arranged the letters in three sections and coda, following my own development as a poet while occasionally providing a window into Allen's work during a given year.

<1976-1979 "Getting to Know You": Allen's continuous encouragement, creating publishing openings and connecting me with other poets, my own initial amazement that he found my work promising, my struggle to understand how to build a friendship and personal understanding with a poet whom I'd built into a legendary figure—gradually addressing my own pretentious claims and neurotic formations, discarding the image I'd made and learning to meet a friend. The "poetry business" that would characterize our later correspondence does begin around 1977 with news of my winning the Pushcart Prize, but Allen included my work in his selections of younger poets in *New Directions Anthology* #37 (1978) and *City Lights Journal* #4 (1978), and the process of editing my work for the proposed City Lights "three-in-one" book (Antler, Andy Clausen, and me) begins in the latter part of this section.

    This was the period when I had completed my U of Michigan degree (1974) after dropping out and working in factory from 1970-1973, hired as night ghetto school custodian 1973-1975, and, during the 1976-1979 years, serving as pool attendant at a school for mentally disabled students. I remained a custodian and developed my *Big Scream*/Nada Press publishing other poets in 1974; the magazine has completed its print run with issue #60 as of this year, 2021. My daughter Anne was born in 1975; I had achieved some local fame as a young poet and met Allen briefly at the 1973 National Poetry Festival, where I got his address and saved it for a time when my poetry would possibly be worthy of his gaze. My *Stars* chapbook was the entry to the correspondence. During this period of letters, I was 28-31 years old.

<1980-1989 "Building a Poetry Life": My initial response to the 1980 Naropa visit was uninhibited exhilaration, but shortly after that, the letters move into the shared poetry business that would characterize most of the correspondence from that point on. This group includes Allen's shepherding of my growth to fuller understanding of the life I had chosen years before: the 1982 Kerouac Conference, the 1986 visit to Boulder for Andy Clausen's series, the 1987 Objectivist Conference with Allen and Carl Rakosi, the 1988 visits to New York for appearance in Allen's Brooklyn series, and to accept the American Academy/Institute of Arts & Letters Award for my *On the Bridge*, all experiences we shared. The decade ends with my suggestion and initial plans to Allen and Anne Waldman for what would eventually become the 1990 Naropa Ecology and Poetics Conference.

<1990-1996 and Coda: Young Poets for Scream, Beats & Rebel Angels, Spring Readings for Gelek Rinpoche, The Intense Finale: Beginning with the letters associated with the 1990 Naropa Eco-Conference, this group includes our dual trajectory in developing cultural diversity in our classes, and follows with Allen's continuing pattern of sending me young poets' work for *Big Scream*, the 1993 reading and lecture at Grand Rapids Community College, and the 1994 Beats and Other Rebel Angels Conference at Naropa. It ends on an intense note: the script of Allen's letter of recommendation so that I can enter PhD program, my letters on his last three performances at Michigan (spring 1994, 1995, 1996), my letter thanking him for tender care of Karen Ide after Chris Ide's death, and for his kindness in offering me a place at Beats & Other Rebel Angels Conference. The Coda ends the collection with my 1997 letter to Jim Cohn, describing the "Closing the Bardo" ceremony replacing what would have been his fourth straight annual performance at Hill Auditorium, Ann Arbor; I also included a section of notes on what Allen taught me, a bit of perspective written during my 1998 visit to Naropa.

Other notes:

Titles in italics replace underlined book titles in letter scripts; titles of individual poems, also underlined in manuscript, are signified here with quotation marks.

I have corrected typos when appropriate (e.g. foreword, not forward—for the Foreword to *Quiet Lives*).

Appendix B

Allen Ginsberg Published in *Big Scream* / Nada Press Chapbooks

"Dear David: hazy in steamer lounge," in *Big Scream* 20 (1985). The "postcard poem."

"It's All So Brief" and "No Longer" in *Big Scream* 21 (1986).

"Cadillac Squawk" in *Big Scream* 23 (1986).

"Poetry, Violence, and the Trembling Lambs." *Big Scream* 24 (1987). Reprint of early essay. Cover photo of Allen and Peter Hale by Steve Miles.

"I Went to the Movie of Life," in *Big Scream* 27 (1989)

Thanks. Chapbook by David Cope and students, welcoming Allen to Grand Rapids Community College. February 19, 1993.

"American Sentences" and "In The Benjo," in *Big Scream* 32 (1993). Allen Ginsberg cover photo by Darlene Kazmarczyk.

Allen Ginsberg: Shared Dreams, Some Roots & Later Leaves, Some Sources & Descendents 1994. Course book for David Cope's class on Allen's later poems at the Beats and Other Rebel Angels Conference, Naropa 1994.

"After Europe! Europe!" and "The Bonfire (Rescued at the Last Minute)," in *Big Scream* 34 (1996). Poems from 1958 and 1957, respectively.

Big Scream 35: *Sunflowers & Locomotives: Songs for Allen.* Cover photo of Allen on 12th St. fire escape by Christopher Funkhouser, back cover photo of Allen and Peter Hale by Steve Miles. Mementos, elegies and paeans for Allen after his death, plus xerox of Allen's handwritten lyrics and arrangement of Blake's "Nurse's Song" (1997).

Appendix C

David Cope published or awarded per Allen Ginsberg's Editing / Nominations

"Crash," published in *The Pushcart Prize II: Best of the Small Presses*. Ed. Bill Henderson. Yonkers: Pushcart Press, 1977. Nominated by Allen.

Five poems in *City Lights Journal* #4. Ed. Mendes Monsanto. San Francisco: City Lights, 1978. Selected by Allen.

Two poems and "Fragments" in *New Directions* #37. Ed. James Laughlin. New York: New Directions, 1978. One of several poets selected in "Ginsberg's Choice."

Featured poet in Allen's January 7, 1980 lecture on poetics. Naropa Institute (now University).

Poet and lecturer at Naropa Institute, 1980. Invited by Allen.

Allen's Guest at The Jack Kerouac Conference, Naropa University, Boulder, CO, 1982.

Foreword. *Quiet Lives*. Totowa: Humana, 1983. Allen recommended David's work to publisher Thomas Lanigan, who published six of David's books from 1983 to 2003. This connection is owed to him.

Three poems in *Friction 5/6: Obscure Genius ,*. Ed. Allen Ginsberg and Randy Roark. Boulder: Laocoon, Winter 1984.

Award in Literature. The American Academy and Institute of Arts and Letters, for David's book, *On the Bridge*. New York, 1988. Nominated by Allen.

20 poems in *Clear Seeing Poetics*. Ed. Allen Ginsberg. Unpublished massive course pack book for Allen's classes at Brooklyn College.

"Sirens & Flashing Lights Stop." *Poems for the Nation: A Collection of Contemporary Political Poems*. Ed. Allen Ginsberg, with Andy Clausen and Eliot Katz. New York: Seven Stories, 2000.

Foreword to *Quiet Lives. Deliberate Prose: Selected Essays 1952-1995*. By Allen Ginsberg. Ed. Bill Morgan. New York: HarperCollins, 2000.

Appendix D

David Cope Poems read by Allen Ginsberg in his 7 January 1980 lecture/reading (Basic Poetics), Naropa Institute (University), Boulder, CO.

Note: Titles without quotation marks are complete poems; those enclosed in quotation marks are discrete sections from multi-sectional poems, collaged pieces.

Keys

EP red: *Early poems*, red notebook
EP blue: *Early poems*, blue notebook,
Clouds: *The Clouds*. Grand Rapids: Free Press, 1974, 1975. Chapbook.
Stars: *The Stars*. Grand Rapids: Nada, 1976. Chapbook.
ND 37: *New Directions Anthology* #37. Ed. J. Laughlin et al. New York: New Directions, 1978,
QL: *Quiet Lives*. Foreword by Allen Ginsberg. Totowa: Humana, 1983.
OTB: *On the Bridge*. Totowa: Humana, 1986.

Sources

Clouds	
"The ancient bandleader" [Flashing Air 3]	Clouds 6
"All night the snow fell" [Flashing Air 4]	Clouds 6
The Line Up	Clouds 7 / QL 2
"Nuance" (?)	
The Ferry	Clouds 8
Empty Street	QL 3
"All the hip people hurry into bars"	EP red, marked, unpaginated
The Evidence	Clouds 12
January	Clouds 14
Prophecies 1 & 2 [The Prophecies]	Clouds 15
"Thousands of opera goes spill into the street"	Clouds 16
"We Sleep"	Clouds 16
"Music"	Clouds 16
"Ornament"	Clouds 17
"Sleepy Plaza"	[Clouds 18 or 19?]
The Riot	Clouds 20
"Cemetery"	Clouds 21
"*Big Scream*"	EP blue, marked, unpaginated
Down on the Farm	QL 5
"Traffic Island"	EP red, marked, unpaginated
"Walking, driving, everything is business"	Stars 1 / EP red, marked, unpag.
This is an AMERICAN POEM	Stars 3 / EP red marked, unpag. / ND 47
Two old friends stand [appear] in a crowd	Stars 4 / EP red marked, unpag.
Baseball	Stars 5
"An old woman leans against a tree"	Stars 7 / EP red marked, unpag. / ND 48

"Evening" [The River]	Stars 8 / EP red marked, unpag.
Crash	Stars 9
"Lines of headlights"	Stars 11
"The Evening Streets"	Stars 15
Twilight [Detroit]	Stars 16
Lunch Hour	Stars 17
Asphalt	Stars 18
The Beating	Stars 26
"The hat, the cane"	Stars 28
"There [three?] drivers wait for their load"	Stars 32
The Morning Sun	Stars 38
End of the Shift	QL 29
Moonlight in West Virginia	OTB 23
The Old Black Woman	
Arlington	
The Crypt	
Clouds	

Notes

1976-1979: Getting to Know You

Page 18: October 8, 1976 letter: misdated 1967 in manuscript.

Page 19: December 10 date fixed to letter by Allen's secretaries must refer to filing date; Allen sent reply re sending mag to Creeley on same date, so I'm guessing my letter must have been written at least a week or two before December 10.

Pages 19-20: January 3 1977. Manuscript letter is misdated to January 3, 1976. Subject matter indicates this letter was written in Jan 1977: Allen's first letter to me was written on March 18, 1976 (after the presumptive date of this one), and *Go*, the chapbook Allen refers to in the letter, was the follow-up to *Stars*, printed late in 1976; Allen would have gotten it early in 1977—an appropriate date for this letter.

Pages 20-21: Jan. 1977. Manuscript letter is misdated to Jan 14, 1976. Subject matter indicates this letter was written in Jan 1977. My sense of Andy Clausen's work here is off-base. The National Beat Poetry Foundation has rightfully named him New Generation Beat Poet Laureate for life.

Page 21: Jan. 14, 1977. Manuscript letter is dated to Jan. 10, 1977. This date is incorrect, because Allen's previous letter (originally dated to Jan. 14) announces that he's sending Andy Clausen's new book, and this "Jan. 10" letter of mine is responding to Andy's book. The time frame doesn't add up.

Pages 23-26: Jan. 25, 1977, the "American Airlines letter": Allen's correction of my generalizations with evidence elsewhere in my poem: "Turks + cows are more live." The correction contains a peculiar irony in that I was referring to "a thousand Turks buried alive" and "cows dropping in their tracks" (two current news items), both images "live" only in that they're not generalized or abstract. See "The Rose" in *Quiet Lives*, page 20.

Pages 26-28: Feb 10 1977. Originally marked c. 1976, this letter is misdated via internal evidence: *Mind Breaths*, subject of my response, was not published until 1977; it also refers to Allen's "American Airlines" letter (here recalled as Pan Am Airlines letter) of January 25, 1977, wherein he speaks of "woodshedding with 18 yr old poet friend, both of us reading 6-10 hrs. a day." Allen notes the "mature porphyry-voiced" pages of "Jerusalem" and recommends Bloom's notes and other standard reference works of Blake scholarship, then explains the Four Zoas in brief. Because the date of that letter is later than the one ascribed to this one, I suggest the date of this letter is some time following the January 25, 1977 letter from Allen.

<reference to the tale of Vainamoinen and Joukahainen in the Finnish *Kalevala*, first explained to us by Ted Enslin at the 1973 National Poetry Festival, Allendale, Mi. Allen was a major draw at

this conference; I was a 25 year old poet invited to sit in because I had won a local poetry contest.

<This letter is best characterized as a set of youthful indiscretions, thinking I knew much more than I did. It does try to come to terms with my own mental formations in the PS. Given my earlier pronouncements in this same letter, the boastful comment is absurdly improper in retrospect, but it is also a grave misreading of both the tragic elements and the "mountain zen lesson" in *The Dharma Bums*. My comments re Gary Snyder are also borne of ignorance, though well-meant: when I met Gary and later worked with him on the "Declaration of Interdependence." at Naropa Institute (now University), I discovered not a "wild man" but a master scholar of the wilderness and of the balances necessary for humans to live in accord with the world we have inherited.

Pages 28-29: This letter was undated and there were no clear internal references to place it in context of the letter stream, yet the Raleigh poem [long since abandoned per my published oeuvre] noted as attached to this letter was written in May of 1977, so I am placing it in that part of the letter stream here.

Pages 30-31: March 27, 78. "Meeting you last weekend": Allen had asked me to introduce myself to him, should I be present at one of his readings, and I did so at a Washington D. C. reading that Sue, my daughter Anne and I attended with our friends Gary and Lin Schmidt. Afterwards, we went to party somewhere in the city, where he showed me FBI files obtained through FOIA— we went through the FBI correspondence on what to do about Detroit and Ann Arbor radicals—an agent was told not to buy pig's blood, which he thought could be used by operatives dressed as hippies, to throw the blood on older "respectable" protesters in front of TV cameras, etc. Also news that the *Michigan Daily* was infiltrated during the time I was on campus. "Watching Allen Read" poem typed on same page as contains the above letter. I later abandoned it, but it does capture "his crazy gestures" while reading and noting that his work bears "all of us with him, our loves & hates, our impatience, our silence—thru time to all of you." Poem also insists that he has yet to write "our greatest poem," thus my comment "I know you can do it, & hope you will."

Page 31: June 6, 1978. The request per Duncan is patently absurd—don't know what I must have been thinking during this period. Missing "being there" (Boulder summer session at Naropa): I did, as it turned out, make my way to the sessions in 1980—Allen gave me $100 to cover costs. In PS, the piece I wrote for Ferlinghetti was a youthful retort to his second populist manifesto, "Adieu à Charlot," published along with work by me and my peers, selected by Allen, in *City Lights Journal* #4. As still-angry and thin-skinned youth, I took Lawrence's poem as merely a rebuke to younger poets. My retort and some others in same vein were sent to Ferlinghetti, and it didn't take long for me to realize that I'd overstepped my bounds, missed his larger points, but also that I should be thanking him for including me and my peers in his anthology. Lawrence waited several months and then graciously sent me short card asking what he should do with the manuscript I had sent; I apologized and asked him to recycle it.

Pages 31-32: Detroit Industry Murals postcard, 1978. The poem for Reznikoff has continually popped up in manuscripts etc. and has been revised for later inclusion in my work. *A Need for Tenderness* is short chapbook I had recently published, some of its poems later abandoned, some included in my first book, *Quiet Lives*. *The Clouds* and *Neon Eyes* were early chapbooks, some surrealist experiments later abandoned, some neo-objectivist work later included in my first book as well. Allen would read and comment on some of the poems from these chapbooks in his 7 January 1980 lecture/reading on Basic Poetics at Naropa Institute, available via their online recordings (for complete list and sources of my poems in Allen's lecture, see Appendix D).

Page 32: Anti-nuclear postcard, 1978. Not sure, but I believe the 26-page ms. mailed to City Lights may refer to a group intended for consideration for the "3 in 1" book Allen proposed to Lawrence Ferlinghetti. The City Lights book would initially have included Antler, Andy Clausen, and me, but Ferlinghetti was dubious and Antler eventually withdrew from the project because it would have involved printing his long-lined poems sideways. See pages 235-36, 238, 245-46, 248, and 255 of *I Greet You at the Beginning of a Great Career: The Selected Correspondence of Lawrence Ferlinghetti and Allen Ginsberg 1955-1997*. Ed. Bill Morgan. City Lights, 2015. The 3-in-1 volume was never published, though City Lights did find a way to publish Antler's *Factory*.

Pages 32-33: postmarked Sept. 25, 1979. Letter related to proposed 3-in-1 anthology from City Lights (see earlier note). Note re my position on my generation might not sit well with close friends such as Andy Clausen, yet it does reflect my understanding of the times, at least during this period. My own position became markedly more activist after the election of Reagan, who did his best to destroy all that I believed necessary and hopeful changes.

1980-1989: Building a Poetry Life

Page 38: January 17, 1980 letter. Recollection of Washington D. C. reading (see notes after March 27 and 13 April 1978 letters in previous section), responses by those in my party. My father: quoting 19th century Radical Republican Charles Sumner who was critical of Lincoln as being too moderate toward the South, later one of those who sought to severely punish former confederate states while promoting (to his credit) black empowerment there. Domino theory: right wing domino-effect belief that if one nation in a region came under the influence of communism, surrounding nations would follow. Lebel: Jean Jacques Lebel, French artist, poet, actor, etc., famed for his work in Happenings and for his role in *The Beat Hotel*, film about the cheap hotel where Allen, Gregory, Burroughs, and others found sanctuary in the late 50s/early 60s. Miscarriage: my family was in mourning with friends after our miscarriage when Allen called to invite me to come to Naropa—I was torn between two contrary and intense emotions—intense sorrow at our loss and elation that this opportunity should come my way. When I explained Allen's offer and said I didn't know what to say, Sue told me to accept it. The episode is handled in my paean "Congratulations" published later in Allen's festschrift volume, *Best Minds: A Tribute to Allen Ginsberg*, Ed. Bill Morgan and Bob Rosenthal. New York: Lospecchio, 1986.

Pages 39-40: February 18, 1980. Allen's letter explaining his approach to editing (and honing) my big ms. of poems for the proposed 3-in-1 volume already noted. One of the first references to poet Jim Cohn, whom Allen had introduced to me via mail c. 1979. Jim has been my blood brother, poet whose poems are valentines for all the sufferers, fellow publisher of other poets in our small press magazines, and my most valued correspondent and critic from then until this day. Attachment is recommendation letter, first two paragraphs of which became Foreword to *Quiet Lives*, my first book.

Pages 40-41: c. July 1980. Poem letter misplaced in 1976-1979 series (see 3rd page from end of that series in Stanford pdf). The first of these poems became the final poem of my first book, *Quiet Lives*, which also featured paragraph 1 of Allen's recommendation letter (see Allen to David, Feb. 18 1980) as the Foreword to the book. As for the "God in Heaven" and other crazed ebullience—I had not yet fully divested myself of spook religious upbringing, and both that and the rest should really be taken as indicative of the life-changing experiences I had during my week in Boulder—both the making of lifelong friendships with my peers and strangeness of rivalries and cruelty witnessed among some elders, but also the intense beauty of living my dream and of climbing into the mountains for the first time. The "place" of this week in my career is much more fully discussed in "Moving On: 41 Years of *Big Scream*/Nada Press" (David Cope Interviewed by Jim Cohn), published online in *Big Bridge* 18, Michael Rothenberg, ed. See http://bigbridge.org/BB18/features/BigScream/MOVING_ON.html .

Page 41: likely fall 1980. Like three other letters from the early 80s, this undated letter was misplaced at the end of the 1988-1989 Stanford pdf files. It is indeed a letter that I had thought missing, requesting xerox copies of Marsden Hartley's *Selected Poems*. New York: Viking, 1945. Brandon Press: I'm not sure where that imprint entered my mind; I eventually obtained a good hardcover copy of the book in 2015; the imprint is Viking. Back story: In my summer 1980 visit to Naropa, I delivered two lecture/discussions which were supposed to cover Charles Reznikoff's work, and one reading with Andy Clausen. In the first lecture, I covered much of Reznikoff's work, ending with Rezi's "Kaddish" for his mother, and I talked about the requirements for objectivist/realist presentation. Later, Allen brought me the little-known Hartley poems, pointing out that several of them make good examples of the practice. I read them that evening, and was so taken with them that I decided to devote my second lecture to them. This letter is the missing piece, shewing that I asked Allen for a copy of them; he had Jim Cohn xerox them for me. Later, I wrote and published "Marsden Hartley: Forgotten Classic in *The Poetry Project Newsletter* 116 (November 1985)": 1-2.

Pages 42-44: December 1980. Misplaced letter in Stanford PDF: this undated letter was placed at the end of the 1988-1989 file, yet I immediately recognized it as following directly after John Lennon's death on December 8, 1980. The letter presents my unpublished elegy for Lennon, and details a reading at an "underground coffee house" in Ann Arbor, organized by Al Pearlman. Pearlman was a Naropa student, later a U of Michigan student, who invited me to read at a basement "coffee house" in the Residential College on December 9, 1980. Sue and I made our sojourn to my old alma mater with sorrowful hearts as Lennon's songs played on radio stations all across the state; by the time we arrived, I was an emotional wreck. Pearlman met us, spotted my condition and primed me with liquid courage—a good red wine. I read my working-class factory and apartment cleanup poems to middle class college students with an intensity that surprised me, returning to Grand Rapids the following morning. I mentioned Ken Mikolowski in this letter, and in his of December 30, Allen gives his "regards to Ken Mikolowski."

Page 45: Jan. 1981. In my original transcription of this letter, I had dated it June 81, but this wishing "Happy New Year" seemed incongruous in light of a June date; when I checked the date on the xeroxed postcard message, it became readily apparent that it was Jan, not June. Some repetition in this letter re previous Dec. 30 letter—perhaps he was running too fast. *A Quiet Life* was recently published chapbook of my poems from that period.

Pages 45-47: c. Jan. 1981. Misplaced letter in Stanford PDF: this undated letter was also placed at the end of the 1988-1989 file, but this one is surely from January of 1981. The fact that it mentions that Ferlinghetti was giving up the proposed 3-in-one project follows nicely on Allen's announcement of the same outcome in his of Jan 81; also the mention of Lelia ("something missing (some clue)—she died?") in the same letter shows a close connection in the time sequence. The January 24 date for the "open reading" places this letter in a January time frame, so I placed it here in light of that. The mention of Al Pearlman also links the letter to this period, given my reading in Ann Arbor the month before, sponsored by him; we did not connect after that, and he quickly faded from the poets I corresponded or worked with. Finally, I mention that "I'm 33," which would indicate a 1981 date as well—I was born on 13 January 1948.

Page 48: 1981 April 4. This is an important letter for my work, as the manuscript named above was further revised over the period of the next year, and was published in March of 1983 as *Quiet Lives*, my first book, with a Foreword by Allen (same recommendation letter first paragraph named here.) Charlie Ross and Mary Lu Banta were two Naropa students I'd met during my summer 1980 visit, and she hailed from same part of Michigan as me.

Pages 48-49: 1981 Dec. 1. Festival was in 1973, not 1972. The walk to midsummer bonfire with the Oppens is a treasured memory.

Pages 49-50: Jan 7, 82 7 AM. with attached copy of December 9, 1981 letter to *Time*. This letter (not the attachment) was dated Jan. 7 '81 by one of the office staff. It was plainly from January of 1982, responding to my request of December 1, 1981, so I have changed the date to 1982. Evidence: the requests for addresses for Lanigan and Oppen, answered in Allen's letter, and my comment on Peter Orlovsky's poems, which elicited response by Allen. Attached letter to *Time* magazine was Allen's response to their misquoting him about younger poets he appreciated, notably printing my name as "Pope," not "Cope."

Pages 50-51: 1982 Jan. 9. Unsure whether the radio show noted at WFMU was ever presented there; Bob Rixon, poet later known as "DJ Rix," would have hosted it, but at this 2016 date, he is deceased. I had forgotten, too, that the *Time* article brought loads of reporters; in their letters to the editor, they chose to print my mother's corrective letter—surname Cope, not *Time* reporter's misprint, Pope—rather than printing Allen's generous note to them, reproduced above. I have no recollection of these interviews, but this paragraph showed a bit of the humor associated with interactions with journalists.

Pages 51-52: 1982 May 28. This letter shows undue colloquial familiarity and a lack of awareness of time frames for attending a major conference, as well as of the levels of work Allen would have been doing during these months. It also misses a major point about the Kerouac Conference. It is, of course, good that the art move on from the work of Allen's generation, but this conference was a big way of reminding the world of Jack's major contributions to American prose style, a watershed gathering of the surviving beats to celebrate his life and theirs during their later years, and providing a forum for the eventual worldwide canonization of Kerouac's work in literature: there were many worldwide scholars and lit. journalists there, in addition to editors, publishers, academics, and old beats and youthful types who could either provide comment or spread that word. Beyond this, Allen was once again graceful to this upstart poet: I came to the conference as his "honored guest," stayed at Tom Swartz's house, sang "My Girl" with poet friend Jim Ruggia at giant party while the come-ons were happening at a torrid pace around us.

Page 52-53: after July 2 (last date of Kerouac Festival), before Nov. 1982. *Big Scream*: #15, the second issue of that year. Twilight Tribe—younger local poets more devoted to readings than publication—my claim to have helped them is overstated here—I read with them and dialogued about publication, but they were singularly self-driven. Jack Kerouac *On the Road* Conference, June 30-July 2, 1982; I was Allen's "honored guest" but had no planned reading (likely because I was so late in affirming I could come). Peter Orlovsky gave up half of his reading time, so I opened for Peter and for the great working man poet Jack Micheline to an afternoon audience of 400, afterwards earning a congratulations from him for my performance. The Clash—*Combat Rock* tour; my friend Bill Breidenfield was connected to the local promoters and offered to get me in to see them after the show (on basis of my relationship to Allen), but I declined. Old English—the opening lines of "Eard Stapa" became part of my quick oral lesson on the evolution of English, also including the opening 30 lines to Chaucer's "Prologue"—recited in all my Shakespeare classes when introducing the Early Modern English of the plays. Around 1995, I took a graduate class in Old English as part of my post-masters degree work at Western Michigan University.

Pages 53-54: 1982 Nov. 16. The reading tour I spoke of never came off. The selected poems I refer to in this letter is the text of *Quiet Lives*, which was in a sense a selection of my poems from the early period of my work. Published March 15, 1983—with informal book launch at my reading with Andy Clausen and Antler, introduced by Allen, 67th Street YMCA, NYC. Hello to Peter Orlovsky—like Peter, I have always been deeply committed to working on the land, to healing the earth I live on via good organic practices such as use of mulch. "BIG anthology of my generation's poems/ poets" continues my feeling that my generation of poets—later dubbed "postbeat"—were/are significantly different than our elders, despite continuing the lineages that they extended. Early reference to anthology, which would become *Nada Poems* in 1988.

Page 54: Charleville, Dec. 21, 82. This and the "postcard poem" written me from China on November 11, 1984 (published as poem in *Big Scream* 20 Feb. 15, 1985 and later as "Poem" in *Wait Till I'm Dead: Uncollected Poems*. Ed. Bill Morgan. Grove, 2016, page 185) are my two favorite letters from Allen, with the "American Airlines" letter of January 25, 1977 a close third.

Pages 54-55: between Dec 21, 1982 and March 12, 1983. Misdated letter in file [ca. 1984]: reference to previous Charleville postcard and upcoming March 1983 readings/book launch for *Quiet Lives* in Hoboken and New York place it between Dec 21, 1982 and March 12, 1983. Notice for "Big Reading" 3/14/83—Monday 8 p.m. at Unicorn Bookstore, Washington St, Hoboken, featuring David Cope, Jim Cohn, Nina Zivancevic, and Lorna Smedman. My trip to NJ/NYC began at James Ruggia / Sharon Guynup's apartment on Willow Street; Andy Clausen came down to join us and there are some fine photos of all of us except Lorna, taken on Hoboken streets by Sharon Guynup. The Washington Street reading happened on Monday, and my reading with Andy and Antler occurred on Tuesday; I flew out Wednesday.

Page 55: 1983 May 14 AG, in Allen's hand. Tom Lanigan, my editor and publisher at Humana, made up three leatherbound presentation copies of my *Quiet Lives*, one for me, one for Allen (whose foreword introduced me), and one for himself. I asked that a second paperback copy be sent to Allen for a "working copy" of the book. Records—he gave me a copy of *First Blues* LP when I visited, inscribing it "For David Cope in New York March 15, 1983 Welcome to the Apple Allen Ginsberg 437 E 12 St Apt 23." Spanish poets—I was working at a largely Latinx elementary school, Hall School (now Cesar Chavez Elementary) in Grand Rapids, and began writing on Spanish and Spanish American poets for *La Voz*, ed. José Flores. The only actual piece that I recall publishing there was my translation of José Gautier Benítez's poem, "Puerto Rico!" Eventually, I would translate two of Lope de Vega's sonnets (*Rimas Humanas* I and *Rimas Sacras* II), and a short and lovely lyric on the Noche de San Juan. Jepsen—a Boulder poet and translator who gave me his book of translations of German expressionist poets, *Expressionismus*; I found the work impressive and published some of it. Two jobs: from the mid-seventies through about 1984, I periodically worked weekends cleaning ghetto apartments for a landlord who was a childhood friend; my regular custodial job did not pay enough to cover my family's expenses.

Pages 56-57: 10/30/83. I eventually gave up on translating all of *Romancero Gitano*, though I still love that book. Allen did not, of course, give me Dylan's address. Rixon never published a complete full length book, though he continued to write and publish superb short poems right up until his death a few years ago. I picked up on Trungpa's *Cutting Through Spiritual Materialism* and the spiritual biographies of Milarepa and Marpa when in Boulder to read in Andy Clausen's series in 1986, all three of these books very important to my later development.

Pages 57-58: 5 Nov 83 AG, in Allen's hand. Emerson's poem, "Ode, Inscribed to William H. Channing," is important for its most famous line, "things are in the saddle / and ride mankind."

Page 58: Likely from 1983 or 1984. Letter from 1988-1989 Stanford pdf, misplaced: This is certainly not from 1988-1989. I'm unsure what the "booklet" was, but my chapbook production was heaviest during the early 80s. The letter is likely from late 1983 or early 1984, after the

December 27, 1983 Buffalo propane explosion that killed seven. Click on the link for information on that: https://en.wikipedia.org/wiki/1983_Buffalo_propane_explosion

Page 59: after 11/16/83 and before 1/18/84. Misdated letter [ca. 1985]: references to Guillén and Pessoa in Allen's 11/16/83 letter are responded to here; thus this letter must date after 11/16/83 and before 1/18/84. References to kids at Hall School (many Latinx kids): I left Hall School in 1984 because of an abusive administrator and spent the next seven years as head custodian and as of 1986, both custodian and evening adjunct English instructor at Grand Rapids Junior College (now Community College). My poetry research interests broadened there, as I had access to Grand Rapids Public Library and the college's library. Emily Dickinson—eventually I became deeply fond of Dickinson's work, and employed it in my teaching as well.

Pages 60-61: 2-10-84. *Hall School Poems*—small chapbook of 4th-6th graders' poems chosen and edited by me after classroom visits. Principal provided funds to publish 500 of each issue, that younger siblings could see the writings of their elder brothers and sisters, and to share with other elementary schools in the district. *Grand Rapids Press* published a story on me based on this, and later I organized an in-house show involving these poems, current dances to then-popular songs, etc., which was aired on local WZZM-TV Sunday show highlighting aspects of local culture. DIA reading organized by George Tysh—though it was a March date, there was a huge snowstorm then, and I read to about 10 people who showed up; I was fortunate, however, to pick up a hardcover of Edwin Denby's *Collected Poems*. Vietnamese friends: Suzanne and I had sponsored a family of Vietnamese refugees, and we helped them adjust to life in America. Their six children later all graduated from college, and they remain our friends to this day.

Pages 61-62: March 23, 1984. *Friction 5/6: Obscure Genius* , ed. Allen Ginsberg and Randy Roark, eds. Swartz: Tom Swartz, Muskegon native son featured with me and others in "Ginsberg's Choice" in *New Directions* 37 (1978). Swartz became a good friend and taught me the caveats for mountain climbing, ascending Long's Peak with me and others in 1982. He later married poet Elizabeth Kerlikowske and returned to Kalamazoo, Mi.

Page 62: April Fools Day 84. Allen's lament re *Friction 5/6: Obscure Genius* issue. Co-editor Randy Roark had left copious blank space in my and Bobby Meyers' selections; I had submitted plenty of top drawer material to fill those pages, thus Allen's concern. I remain very proud to have been a part of that edition.

Page 65: November 11, 1984. This "postcard poem" was published in *Big Scream* 20. Later, it would be translated by Zhang Ziqing of the Institute of Foreign Literature/Nanjing University, and it appears in his study, *A History of 20th Century American Poetry* (3 vols.), published in Chinese in Beijing, 2019. Zhang notes his source as my *Big Scream* 20. It has also appeared under the title "Poem" in *Wait Till I'm Dead: Uncollected Poems* by Allen Ginsberg (ed. Bill Morgan. Grove, 2016.).

Page 63-64: Nov. 84. This letter solicits permission to publish Allen's "postcard poem": Ruggia and 40 sheep: James found a way out of this awkward situation without antagonizing his hosts. Monticello: I was much impressed with the site, but nonplussed the guide by asking where the slave quarters were located, later getting an answer. I am told that the roles of the slaves—ignored when I was there, at least until the subject was broached—have since been included. My poem "Monticello" from the 1985 visit was one of those that took years to be fleshed out; it is found in 1990's *Fragments from the Stars*.

Page 64: Jan 14 1985. "Searching for the next generation": this search begins around this period but only begins to bear fruit when Allen sends me the work of Chris Ide, and when I begin teaching full time, in my first semester as full-time prof (fall, 1991) meeting my student and Romanian dissident's daughter, Carmen Bugan, who has gone on to a fine career as poet, scholar, and memoirist, winning awards and being feted and translated on both sides of the Atlantic. Second book: *On the Bridge*, was not published in the summer of 1985, rather in 1986. It would win a 1988 Award in Literature from the American Academy/Institute of Arts & Letters (now American Academy of Arts & Letters).

Page 65: Feb 85. Book signing: Allen signed copies of his *Collected Poems 1947-1980* for two hours at the Detroit Art Institute, later taking dinner and in the evening, doing lengthy reading at the same. He asked me to keep him company during the signing; he was courteous, thoughtful, kind with every person who brought a book to be signed, whether his new one or some old treasured copy of *Howl* or *Kaddish* or other Allen book. Occasionally I would join in the conversation, but mostly learned by observing his gracious behavior with many different lovers of his work.

Page 65-66: May 85. "First thought, best thought" was the current poetics motto being repeated, often without ever critically appraising what it meant, by many students of poetry during this period. I was troubled by it, and wanted clarifications. "Eard-Stapa" : Old English "The Wanderer," which I learned to recite in the original so that poetry students and others could get a feel for the power of the OE stressed line and, of course, for its beauty and pathos.

Page 66: 2/4/86. Computer poem scripts enclosed with this letter: "Written in My Dream by W.C. Williams," "It's All So Brief," "No Longer." See his next letter—Allen had to withdraw the first of these from *Big Scream* because *Poetry* (Chicago) had accepted the poem on condition that it be unpublished.

Page 67: Feb 86. Hartley essay: My "Marsden Hartley: Forgotten Classic" essay was lead story in *The Poetry Project Newsletter* 116 (November 1985).

Page 68: Mars 86. "A new world…" (from WCW's "Daphne and Virginia") and "Eternity's in love…" from William Blake's *Proverbs of Hell*, these two serving as final lines of my "Horns of Light" in *On the Bridge* (1986).

Page 71: Sunday morn Aug 3 86. Allen's "Cadillac Squawk" was published in *Big Scream* 23 (1986). Steve: Steven Taylor, poet and guitarist for The Fugs and for Allen. Steinbeck: John Steinbeck Jr., whom I met after Allen introduced him to the Vietnam War poems in *Quiet Lives* (he served in Nam). Hartley: *Collected Poems*, not *Complete Poems*,

Page 72: 14 Dec. 1986. Chris Ide: incandescent young poet in Kerouacian tradition, burned like a Roman candle and died of heroin overdose in 1994. "…bring a whole new generation alive": planned objectivist conference at Naropa Institute, summer 1987.

Page 74: Mars 31 87. Baby girl: my daughter Jane, born 5 March. "Solar greenhouse": I ripped broken roof off wooden shed in backyard and opened space in south wall and east wall for windows; designed windowed roof angled for maximum solar exposure, later insulated walls & put in interior boarded walls, built massive shelves for plants, pots, & saucers.

Page 74: 7 6 87. Likely a note left on the table with key at apartment we shared in Boulder during 1987 Objectivist Conference, highlights for me including reading with Carl Rakosi, breakfast with Allen and Carl, and evening spent singing Dowland and Campion songs with Steven Taylor as a young woman massaged Allen's aching leg, he singing bass. That evening is subject of the third stanza of "for allen," poem I wrote on learning of his death in 1997 and published in *Silences for Love* (Humana, 1998).

Page 74: 1987 Aug 3. Follow-up to Objectivist Conference—Allen was injured trying to restrain Peter Orlovsky during one of Peter's "mad againe" moments (see note to last letter, "Allen's aching leg.") Concern in PS: Allen was troubled by Peter's condition, but also I worried that he would try to keep moving at same pace he had carried on earlier, thus "don't try to do too much."

Page 77: 8 28 87. "Be careful the way you tread": ironic note in light of Chris Ide's death 7 years later.

Pages 77-78: 10 30 87. Transitional time in my worklife: head custodian at GRJC Main/North Building (200 rooms, 36 custodians plus trades staff) by day, adjunct English faculty by night. Handouts: Lockwood was teaching sophomore creative writing class, thus the introduction to contemporary poetics, and Lyric Tradition handout was for Van Haitsema's sophomore poetry class (traces move from Reawakening to Latin/Roman poesy, Peasant Dance Traditions, Neo-Latin hymns, Goliard poets > Provencal Troubadours >Four separate national traditions: Italy (Dante Boccaccio Petrarch etc. with stanza forms; England (Chaucer, Wyatt and Surry, Sidney and Spenser [arrow to them from Petrarch], Shakespeare, Byrd, Campion, Dowland [arrow to them from later Italian writers]; France: Sonnets, chansons (Villon, Marot, Ronsard—arrow from them to Chaucer); Germanic Traditions (not specified, but arrows leading to all the English poets).

Page 78: c. Dec. 87. More initial preparation for visit to Allen's poetry class at Brooklyn College in Spring of 1988. I don't believe Steven Taylor and I actually performed any of the songs in my session, but the letter certainly indicates my deeper interest in the English ayre, lute songs.

Pages 78-79: 1 15 88. *Big Scream*: 1987 issue, #24, with Steve Miles photo of Allen and Peter Hale. It likely was printed later than I'd hoped; there were two issues in 1988, neither of which featured Allen's work, thus the guess.

Page 79: 2 5 88. Continuing queries as pre-prep for April visit to Brooklyn College. Du Bellay: my admiration for the Pleiade poets continues to this day. I published adaptations of Du Bellay's "Songe" (from *Antiquitez de Rome*) and Pierre de Ronsard's Sonnet 26 from the second book of *Sonnets Pour Helene* as late as 2003, in *Turn the Wheel* (Humana). The poems seemed more significant in light of the 9/11 tragedy. 300 lb. cart: life-changing event—I snapped a muscle in my calf, and my personal doctor later responded, "you're not 23 anymore, David—let the young guys do it." Major sign that I should put more into teaching, less into manual labor job.

Pages 79-80: 2/14/88. Peter Hale photo (with Allen): issue #24 of *Big Scream*. Apparently a young and old man posing together affectionately must have been setting off alarms in some places of the country. No problem for me.

Pages 79, 80-81: 2/14/88 and 2/23/88. Two letters prepping me for my visit to NYC to speak at Brooklyn College in Living Poets Series. When I actually arrived, Allen & I were both exhausted from our respective busy lives—at one point we slept 20 hours straight, waking together every few hours for tea or to talk, then falling asleep again. A high point of the trip was our dinner at Christine's, where we had light meals & big German chocolate cake together as Allen signed autographs for excited children of Danish visitors to U.S.A. who sat across the restaurant & recognized him. Also read, per my letter of the 19th, at Court Tavern in New Brunswick.

Page 81: March 25 88. I worked on this anthology as early as 1983 (see my May 14 letter of that year). At this point, given the print run, I certainly knew that I had won the $5000 Literature Award from the American Academy and Institute of Arts & Letters (now American Academy of Arts & Letters), and Allen knew it as well, given that he was one of the three judges for the award (along with James Dickey and Irving Howe). This anthology would be named *Nada Poems*, and after attending the ceremony in New York—at which I met both Dickey and Gary Snyder, among many others—I went with Jim Cohn and younger poets Joel Kuszai and Chris Ide to East Lansing, where Kuszai's father was a professor in the computer division at Michigan State University. Professor Kuszai gave us all a 45 minute lesson in how to use the computers, combine our various parts of the final 128 page manuscript into one, develop double columns for Robert Borden's mammoth "Meat Dreams" Vietnam War poem, and format the whole thing for the final 5.5 X 8.5 book. We later provided screened photos of many of the poets and instructions as to how we wanted the cover, and the printer took care of that and the rest. As a nominal *Big Scream* 25, it was one of two issues released that year. Eileen Myles didn't get her work in by deadline, so her poems were published in *Big Scream* 26, the other issue that year.

Pages 82-89: 1988 Sept. 12. First mention of ecopoetics conference that would go through many stages of planning and then develop into a form of educational practice adopted later by many colleges and schools across the nation. Gary Snyder and Allen & Peter were already involved with back-to-the-land intentional communities, and Antler & Jeff Poniewaz were in the forefront of ecopoetics both as poetic and activist practices.

Page 89: 9 13 88 3 A.M. Chris Funkhouser and Joel Kuszai were both brilliant young poets and students who helped those of us who were a bit older to adapt to using the computer for typesetting during period when most poets in their thirties and above were still using typewriters. The internet, of course, would not become a factor in the production, distribution and promotion of poetry for several years beyond this period. Chris was a friend of Chris Ide, the young poet whom Allen had sent my way, given that Ide and I were both from the same hometown. Funkhouser would become a lifelong friend, making his way in the field of digital poetics, but he was also my editing partner and computer typist during the marathon four days of interviews that led to the "Declaration of Interdependence," a key document completed from my initial first draft at the 1990 Naropa Eco-Conference (which at this point I was planning with target date of 1991).

Page 89: 1988 Nov. 21. "For Billy" was published in *Fragments from the Stars*. Humana, 1990. Page 96-97. Billy Breidenfield was the younger brother of one of my best childhood friends; he was dying of ALS and, in a whisper, asked me for a prayer. This poem was my response.

Pages 89-90: 1 30 89. Preliminary publicity work for Allen's reading with me at Grand Valley State University, April 20, 1989.

Page 90-91: 3 28 89. *Song of Napalm*—Bruce Weigl's harrowing book about his experiences in Vietnam during that war. Cats: Allen was allergic to cats.

Young Poets for *Scream*,
Beats & Other Rebel Angels,
Spring Readings for Gelek Rinpoche,
The Intense Finale

Page 98: 3/22-90. Two visits to New York in 1988: to read in Allen's class at Brooklyn College, and later, when I learned that I'd won the 1988 Award in Literature from the American Academy and Institute of Arts and Letters for my *On the Bridge*, the first of these visits staying with Allen. Poems from the visits: "Albeniz, Sor & Sanz" (p. 40), "Old Man" (41), "Between Buildings" (66), and "All These Thousands of Windows" (73). Jeff Poniewaz: Jeff could be quite contentious and occasionally suspicious of others, but I found that weathering his storms kept our relationship on an even keel, as both Antler and Jeff were dear friends beyond this sort of thing. Ruggia: his writing of travelogues eventually led to world travel and a good position in the travel industry; he continues to write complex and stirring poems to this day. Joel K.: Kuszai, young poet whose father taught us to use Mac computers at Michigan State U, resulting in one-night whole book data entry and layout of *Nada Poems* anthology; as of this juncture, Joel was in fourth year Latin class at Reed College. Multicultural lit class: I had designed this class as of March, 1990, and in the summer got permission from dean and curriculum committee to offer it, despite the fact that I was still an adjunct instructor. I would be hired full time in 1991, and began teaching the class in September of that year.

Page 98: 4/2/90. New book—*Fragments from the Stars.*, published by Humana, 1990. As of 2016, I'm unsure of whose writings were in the sheaf he sent me.

Page 99: 7 14 90. Request for Allen's CD after 1990 Eco-Conference. "Working with Gary Snyder & Peter Warshall & Bill DeVall": refers to the four day editing and revision sessions I set up with 32 conference members re revising and editing "The Declaration of Interdependence," first draft of which I'd written before coming to conference, eventually becoming a conference document that was later published in *Disembodied Poetics: Annals of the Jack Kerouac School*. Ed. Anne Waldman and Andrew Schelling. Albuquerque: U of New Mexico, 1994. Don: Don Cherry, the jazz trumpeter.

Pages 99-100: 8 27 90. As of 2016, unsure of what the "enclosed ms." involved. Richard Cole: published in *Big Scream* 29 (1990); he did not follow up to continue correspondence or submissions. *Early Poems*,—winning poem of local Dyer-Ives poetry competition, some pre-objectivist pieces & some surrealist prose poems; and *The Blue Notebook*, early prose as noted in letter—have never really sought publication for either of these, not sure they'd warrant publication except as "early work" so scholars could track development from beginning. Second time I mentioned multicultural literature class I was planning—this version involves a different set of authors—I would eventually add *The Life of Milarepa* as a text for study in the second or third year of the class but other texts noted here made for background research. Battle with senator: Senator Levin was against flag burning; I insisted that it was a free person's right to use a mere symbol (which could have many contradictory meanings, depending on one's own experiences) as expression of one's political belief—including flag burning as statement of disgust for US government policy or behavior. "My own homemade spaghetti sauce" should be *our* sauce. I grew roma tomatoes and processed them in hand-cranked Vittorio strainer, but Sue oversaw the entire operation from sauce preparation to cooking through canning.

Page 100: 11 13 90. Full-time: Never did teach the Brit lit course, but eventually spent a few years with intro to philosophy, and later a whole series of other courses, some designed by me (Multicultural Lit, Shakespeare, Women's Studies, etc.). Canton: my reading and radio interview at St. Lawrence University, plus climbing 3 peaks and spending the night camping in mountains. Poems from time with Jim in high peaks show trepidation for upcoming Iraq/Gulf War.

Page 102: 4 24 92. Anne + Jim: Anne Waldman and Jim Cohn came to GRCC and gave readings and lectures, hers on her life in poetry, and on poetry in the Kali Yuga, his on his work with hearing differently abled people in Rochester, NY. They later came to a student apartment and met the students one on one, perhaps Anne's connection with my student Carmen Bugan most significant.

Pages 103-104: 28 Dec 92. Ferguson was published in *Big Scream* #31, which featured Anne Waldman's "Leir." Jim Cohn's research on Pound at St. Elizabeth's: Jim used his ADA credentials to get in and see all of Pound's records at St. Elizabeth's Mental Hospital in Washington, D. C., where Ezra spent 11 years and was only released through the pleas and intercession by Robert Frost, Ernest Hemingway, William Carlos Williams, and others. Funding: I was still learning how to get grants and persuade administrators to combine funds in order to facilitate the appearance of a great poet at the school.

Page 108: 8/4/93. Allen would later combine Foreword from *Quiet Lives* with another paragraph directed to my scholarly work and recommendation to accept me for any program. See Addendum to Form Letter as of 5/23/94 in this group of letters for script of second paragraph of the recommendation. The letter was formally typed, signed and sent to me, and I quickly sent it with my application to the program. During the next three years, I earned 30 credits toward the PhD while teaching 18-19 credit hours at GRCC and raising three children. When Allen passed, I was already worn out by my efforts, and his death gave me pause to reassess the direction my life was taking; at the end of the summer of 1997, I decided to drop out of the PhD program and was hired as an adjunct evening Shakespeare professor at WMU (in addition to my 18 hours at GRCC). I would continue in that role for another seven years, driving the 50 miles to Kalamazoo once weekly before deciding to focus exclusively on the GRCC job.

Page 108-109: likely Jan 1994. My brief but fairly comprehensive description of Allen's 1969 Moratorium Day reading in Ann Arbor may be found in his festschrift volume, *Best Minds: A Tribute to Allen Ginsberg*. Ed. Bill Morgan and Bob Rosenthal. New York: Lospecchio, 1986. Pages 69-70. (Date of reading was Oct. 12th, 1969, not November. This rare book is available at both the Stanford University and University of Michigan Libraries.)

Page 110: 10 April 1994. Request for "The Big Parade" was for *Allen Ginsberg: Shared Dreams, Some Roots & Later Leaves, Some Sources & Descendants,* coursepack for my class there. I also read with Ed Sanders, Sharon Olds, and Galway Kinnell at, I think, Boulder High School. The conference was in many ways the Beats' swan song—the last time the entire still-living crowd of the original surviving Beats would gather together. My desire to spend a little time with Allen at the conference was futile. He was mobbed by poets, well-wishers, hangers-on, and journalist types, and was plainly exhausted. I had been told several years before that he was suffering with progressive heart failure, and felt that I should not add one more voice clamoring for his attention, and thus kept my distance other than brief conversations.

Page 110: 5/23/94. Original blurb: first recommendation letter repeated the text of the Foreword to my *Quiet Lives*. This paragraph was added to it for formal letter of recommendation.

Page 111: 1 June 94. One class at the conference—three *sessions*.

Page 111: 1994 July 21. This is the last letter/attachment in the Stanford pdf files. Allen had originally sent young poet Chris Ide my way, and we had developed a deep relationship. Chris did have a problem with drugs and alcohol, and was not able to attend the *Beats & Other Rebel Angels* conference in Boulder, instead remaining in Chicago. A week or so after returning from the conference, we learned that he had overdosed on heroin, and Sue and I and all of his younger friends met there for the funeral. Allen and Anne Waldman were superb in their support of Morgan Jarema, an old friend of Chris, and of others in Boulder who knew and loved him.

Page 112: 17 Feb 95 During the last three years of his life, Allen read at Hill Auditorium on the University of Michigan) campus in the spring, on behalf of Gelek Rinpoche's Jewel Heart

Community and with cooperation of the university. The 1994 reading featured a magnificent recitation of "Howl," and the following year produced a fine reading of "Kaddish" —despite misgivings he had when we spoke after the reading. In 1996, he introduced new and old poems, and a planned 1997 reading was converted into a "Closing the Bardo" ceremony in which many friends gave readings, performances, brief statements, etc. in memoriam. See my letter to Jim Cohn in the Coda to this collection for a description of that event.

Page 112: 7 April 96. Letter sent to Allen after his 1996 spring reading at Hill Auditorium.

Coda

Pages 118-120: 25 May 97. Letter speaks of "Howl" in 1995 and "Kaddish" in 1996; these dates are incorrect. Allen recited "Howl" at Hill Auditorium in 1994, and "Kaddish" in 1995. The 1996 reading involved other older poems and emphasized some new ones.

Pages 120-123: Excerpt from letter of 19 July 1998. Notes from biographical overview of Allen's life, by Ed Sanders. Perhaps the best biographies of Allen are Michael Schumacher's *Dharma Lion: A Critical Biography Of Allen Ginsberg* (New York: St. Martin's, 1992) and Bill Morgan's *I Celebrate Myself: The Somewhat Private Life of Allen Ginsberg* (New York et al: Viking/Penguin, 2006.)

Index
Names, Titles, Key Events, Publishers, etc.

Alighieri, Dante, 2, 41, 65, 101, 102, 107, 111, 141
   La Vita Nuova, 65
Allen Ginsberg: Shared Dreams, Some Roots & Later Leaves, Some Sources & Descendents, (Cope ed., 1994), 128
Allen, Steve, 60
American Academy/Institute of Arts and Letters, 127, 140, 142, 143, 157
American Book Review, 49
Antler, 32, 39, 45, 52, 53, 55, 67, 69, 71, 77, 81, 82, 84, 85, 87, 88, 91, 98, 99, 101, 106, 109, 110, 121, 126, 137, 138, 142
   Factory, 134
   Last Words, 69, 70, 71
Aristophanes, 22, 41
Attaboy, 17
Aurelius, Marcus, 104
Ball, Gordon, 56, 67
Banta, Mary Lu, 45, 48
Baraka, Amiri, 55, 56
Barnard, Mary, 41
Baudelaire, Charles, 21, 22, 25, 123
   Les Fleurs de Mal, 21
Beach, Mary (photographer), 67
Beats and Other Rebel Angels Conference (Naropa, 1994), 127, 128
Benítez, José Gautier, 138
   "Puerto Rico!" (Cope, trans.), 138
Beowulf, 100
Berg, Peter (founder of bioregionalism) Raise the Stakes, 84
Bernstein, Keith, 76
Berrigan, Ted, 91, 119
Berry, Wendell, 83, 87
Best Minds: A Tribute to Allen Ginsberg (Morgan and Rosenthal, eds.), 145
Bezner, Kevin, 104
Big Fireproof Box (see Kuszai), 99
Black Sparrow Press, 39
Blake, Arthur "Blind", 27
Blake, William, 21, 24, 26, 27, 29, 31, 41, 59, 64, 67, 68, 140

   Complete Poetry & Prose, 23
   Jerusalem, 21, 23, 24, 26
   Milton, 21
   Proverbs of Hell, 140
   Songs of Innocence & Experience, 64
   The Book of Los, 21
   The Book of Urizen, 21
   The Marriage of Heaven and Hell, 21
   Visions of the Daughters of Albion, 38
Bloom, Harold, 23
Blue Wind Press, 45
Bly, Robert, 22
Blyth, R. H., 24
Boccaccio, Giovanni, 141
Borden, Robert, 32, 55, 81, 103, 142
   "Meat Dreams", 142
Boulding, Elise (radical feminist socio-ecologist), 84
Boulding, Kenneth (eco-economics), 83
Breidenfield, William (Bill), 137
Bridges, Pat, 91
Browning, Robert, 52
Bryant, William Cullen, 24
   "Thanatopsis", 24
Bugan, Carmen, 139, 144
Bunting, Basil, 39, 71, 82
Burnett, Chester "Howlin' Wolf", 27
Burr, Debbie (Jewel Heart), 118
Burroughs, William (Billy, Jr.), III, 81
Burroughs, William S., II, 51, 123, 134
Butler, Nate, 61
Byrd, William, 141
Byron, George, Lord Gordon, 24, 82
Cadmus Press, 45
Campion, Thomas, 24, 65, 68, 77, 78, 123, 141
   The Somerset Masque, 77
Cannon, Janet, 55, 81
Cardenal, Ernesto, 68
Carl, John, 42
Carroll, Paul, 55
Catullus, 22, 103
   "The Marriage of Peleus and Thetis" (#64), 103

147

Cendrars, Blaise, 71
   Postcards from America, 71
Chaucer, Geoffrey, 1, 21, 22, 38, 66, 73, 107, 111, 137, 141
   "The Parliament of Fowls", 107
   "The Prologue", 66, 73, 137
   The Canterbury Tales, 107
   Troilus and Criseyde, 107
Chin, Frank, 91
City Lights Press, 6, 25, 26, 31, 32, 38, 39, 40, 126, 155, 156
   City Lights Journal #4, 32, 126, 129, 133, 155
Clapton, Eric, 27
Clausen, Andy, 20, 21, 22, 25, 39, 45, 49, 50, 52, 63, 67, 68, 70, 72, 81, 89, 101, 106, 108, 126, 127, 129, 132, 137, 138
Cohen, Allen (editor of the *San Francisco Oracle*), 88
Cohn, Jim, 39, 42, 51, 52, 55, 61, 65, 71, 76, 77, 81, 82, 83, 84, 85, 87, 98, 99, 100, 101, 102, 103, 118, 120, 127, 134, 137, 142, 144, 145
   Divine April, 65
   Moving On: 41 Years of Big Scream/Nada Press (interview with David Cope), 135, 155
   Napalm Health Spa, 99
Cole, Richard, 99, 100, 143
Commoner, Barry (ecologist and one of the founders of eco-movement), 87
Cope, American Academy/Institute of Arts and Letters Literature Award, 129, 140, 142
Cope, David, 3, 16, 17, 25, 26, 29, 30, 31, 32, 39, 40, 41, 47, 50, 52, 67, 68, 71, 73, 74, 81, 82, 86, 87, 98, 100, 102, 107, 110, 111, 129, 130, 136, 137, 138, 157
   "Marsden Hartley: Forgotten Classic" (essay), 135, 140, 155
   A Need for Tenderness, 31, 133
   A Quiet Life (chapbook), 45, 136
   Big Scream (Cope, ed.), 1, 17, 41, 42, 44, 74, 81, 126, 127, 128, 137, 139, 140, 142, 157
   Coming Home, 101, 102, 103, 104, 107, 108
   Early Poems, 1971-1982 (unpublished), 99, 144
   Fragments from the Stars, 76, 83, 90, 143
   Go, 19, 25, 29, 30
   Nada Poems (Cope, ed.), 82, 88, 89, 137, 142, 143, 157
   Neon Eyes, 31
   On the Bridge (book), 61, 64, 65, 66, 68, 72, 73, 127, 130, 140, 143
   Quiet Lives, 52, 54, 111, 130, 137, 140, 155
   Silences for Love, 107, 110, 111, 141
   Stars, 1, 16, 17, 25, 29, 30, 125, 126, 130
   Sunflowers & Locomotives: Songs for Allen, 120, 128, 157
   The Blue Notebook (early writings, unpublished), 99
   The Clouds, 31, 130, 133
   True Love, 28, 30
   Turn the Wheel, 142
Cope, Jane, 73, 118, 120, 140
Cope, Pushcart Prize, 22, 126, 129, 155, 157
Cope, Suzanne, 134
Cope, William, 118, 120
Coperario, Giovanni (John Cooper), 78
Corso, Gregory, 3, 18, 43, 60
Coyote, Peter, 88
Crane, Stephen, 91
Creeley, Robert, 18, 19, 28, 38, 49, 50, 51, 56, 63, 64, 72
   Mirrors, 60, 64
Dali, Salvador, 77
Damon, S. Foster, 23
   A Blake Dictionary, 23
de Ronsard, Pierre, 141
de Vega, Lope, 55, 138
   Rimas Humanas, 138
   Rimas Sacras, 138
Debs, Eugene, 122
Deep, Said, 81
Deloria, Jr., Vine
   Beyond the Trail of Broken Treaties: An Indian Declaration of Independence, 99
Denby, Edwin, 62, 64, 66, 82, 139
   Collected Poems, 139
Devall, Bill, 99
Dial-a-Poem, 42
Diane Diprima, 5, 11, 85
Dickey, James, 142
Dickinson, Emily, 58, 59, 139
DiMaggio, Ken, 106
Disembodied Poetics: Annals of the Jack Kerouac School (Waldman and Schelling, eds.), 155
Donne, John, 66

Dostoevkski, Fyodor
   Crime and Punishment, 26
   The Brothers Karamazov, 26
Douglas, Lizzie "Memphis Minnie", 27
Dowland, John, 76, 78, 121, 141
Drury, George, 64, 72
du Bellay, Joachim, 73, 79
   Antiquitez de Rome, 79
   Defense et Illustration de la Langue Française, 79
Duncan, Robert, 1, 21, 25, 28, 31, 48, 80, 133
   Roots and Branches, 21
Dylan, Bob, 27, 56, 105, 120, 138
Eard-stapa ("The Wanderer"), 53, 66, 73, 107, 140
Earl of Essex (Richard Deveraux, 2nd Earl of Essex), 102
Eberhart, Richard, 20, 21, 60, 74
Ecopoetics Conference (Naropa Institute, 1990), pre-planning, 142
Eliot, T. S., 38, 60, 61
Elizabeth I (Queen of England), 102
Elmslie, Kenward, 69
Emerson, Ralph Waldo, 58, 138
Enslin, Ted, 22, 132
Erdman, David, 23
Everson, William (Brother Antoninus), 46
   The Residual Years, 46
Fagin, Larry, 24
Faigo, Jane, 51
Felieu, Denise, 24
Ferguson, Jim, 101, 103, 144
Ferlinghetti, Lawrence, 25, 29, 30, 31, 32, 38, 39, 43, 44, 45, 46, 50, 51, 52, 74, 126, 156
   "Adieu à Charlot", 46, 133
   Landscapes of Living and Dying, 46
Ferro Botanica (magazine), 54
Fielder, Cecil, 100
Flores, José, 138
   La Voz (ed. Flores. newspaper), 138
Follett Press, 55
Forman, Dave (Earth First!), 84
Friction 5/6: Obscure Genius, 129, 139, 155
Frost, Robert, 22, 44, 145
Funkhouser, Christopher, 73, 76, 88, 89, 92, 101, 121, 128, 143
Gelek Rinpoche, 118, 119, 127, 143, 145

Genet, Jean, 64
Gens, Jacqueline, 74, 100, 106, 107, 109
Ginsberg and Cope Reading, Grand Valley State University, 1989, 91, 143
Ginsberg Reading, Grand Rapids Community College, 1993, 104, 105, 106, 127
Ginsberg Readings, Hill Auditorium, U of Michigan (1994, 1995, 1996), 127, 145, 146
Ginsberg, Allen (as subject), 17, 25, 29, 30, 39, 49, 58, 60, 63, 86, 104, 110, 125, 128, 129, 139, 146, 155, 156, 157
   "Howl", 103, 109, 118, 121, 140, 146, 157
   "Postcard Poem" (China to Cope 1984), 3, 29, 65, 128, 138
   "Birdbrain" (single recording), 57
   "Kaddish", 98, 112, 118, 140, 145, 146
   "Kral Majales", 31, 43
   "New Democracy Wish List", 104
   "Poetry, Violence, and the Trembling Lambs" (essay), 74, 128
   "September on Jessore Road" (tape recording), 27
   "White Shroud" (poem), 57, 73
   Collected Poems 1947-1980, 140
   Empty Mirror, 16
   First Blues, 27, 56
   Howl, Annotated, 67, 74
   Letter to Eberhart, 20, 21, 60, 74
   Mind Breaths, 26, 42, 125
   Planet News, 109
   Plutonian Ode, 49, 50, 61
   Poems All Over the Place, 38
   The Fall of America, 27
   The Lion for Real (CD), 99, 100
   Wait Till I'm Dead: Uncollected Poems, 138, 139, 156
   White Shroud: Poems 1980-1985, 66, 67
Ginsberg, Cope PhD recommendation letter, 39, 110, 111, 127
Ginsberg, Louis, and Naomi, 122
   Eugene (Brooks), 122
Glass, Philip, 92
Golden, Frederick, 65
   Lyrics of the Troubadours and Trouvères, 65
Gregor Samsa (rock group), 58
Greinke, Eric, 22

Guillén, Nicolás, 58, 59
Guynup, Sharon, 138
Gyuto Monks, 118
Haig, Alexander, 44
Hale, Peter, 79, 118, 120, 128, 142
Hall School Poems, 60, 139
Harjo, Joy, 84
Harrison, George, 29
Harrold, William, 22
Hartley, Marsden, 24, 39, 41, 42, 44, 66, 67, 68, 71, 74
   Collected Poems, 140
   Selected Poems, 125
Hayden, Robert, 43, 99, 118
Hayes, Bruce, 103
Heaney, Seamus, 100
Helms, Jesse, 105
Hemingway, Ernest, 91, 144
Henderson, David, 56
Hernandez, Miguel, 55
Hesiod, 74
Heym, Georg, 55
Hitler, Adolf, 102
Hoffman, Abbie, 88
Hoffmann, Sister Margene (Environmental Task Force of the Niagara Frontier/Love Canal), 87
Holiday, Billie, 27
Hollander, John, 74
Home Planet News (1984), 62
Homer, 22, 105
Hoover, J. Edgar, 104
Horace (Quintus Horatius Flaccus), 69, 71
Howe, Irving, 142
Hughes, Langston, 99
Humana Press, 48, 49, 50, 51, 55, 100
Hurt, John "Mississippi John, 27
Ide, Christopher, 66, 67, 70, 71, 72, 76, 88, 103, 111, 118, 120, 121, 127, 139, 140, 141, 142
Ide, Karen, 10, 111, 127
Jarema, Morgan, 146
Jefferson, Lemon Henry "Blind Lemon", 27
Jefferson, Thomas, 63
Jepsen, Tom, 52, 55, 138
   Expressionismus, 138
Johnson, Robert (American bluesman), 27
Johnson, Robert (English composer, lutenist), 78
Jonson, Ben, 101
Joplin, Janis, 27
Jung, Philip, and Joni, 119
Kabir, 105
Katz, Eliot, 61, 81, 129
Keats, John, 106
Keeler, Greg, 84, 85, 91
Kennedy, John F., 118
Kenner, Hugh, 62
   The Pound Era, 62
Kerlikowske, Elizabeth, 55, 81, 139
Kerouac Conference (Naropa, 1982), 51, 88, 127, 129, 136, 137
Kerouac, Jack, 21, 24, 51, 60, 61, 105, 123, 137
   Big Sur, 77
   On the Road, 21, 28, 137
   The Book of Dreams, 27
   The Dharma Bums, 27, 133
Keynes, Geoffrey, 23
King, Jr., Martin Luther, 91, 99
   Why We Can't Wait, 91
Kinnell, Galway, 47, 73, 145
Kowit, Steve, 56
Kraut, Rochelle, 24
Kupferberg, Tuli, 38
Kuszai, Joel, 88, 98, 99, 142
   Big Fireproof Box (ed. Chris Funkhouser and Chris Ide), 99
Lanigan, Thomas (Cope's editor and publisher), 49, 50, 55, 59, 68, 82, 83, 99, 100, 104, 108, 129, 138
Lao-Tze, 105
Laughlin, James, 17, 25, 26, 29, 30, 129
Lawrence, D. H., 24, 39
Lebel, J. J., 38, 134
Ledbetter, Huddie "Leadbelly", 27
Lennon, John, 44, 125
Lerner, Eric, 32
Levertov, Denise, 47
Levin, Senator Carl, 144
Levy, Morris (Mendel Levergunt), 122
   Eleanor, 122
   Max, 122
   Naomi, 122

Sam, 122
Lewis, Joel, 64, 74
Lhalungpa, Lobsang, 64
Lichter, Paul, 61
Lockwood, Walt, 78, 141
Lorca, Federico García, 56, 99
   Romancero Gitano, 56
Lowell, Robert, 24, 38, 42, 91
Machado, Antonio, 55
Managh, Geoffrey, 112
Mariah, Paul, 64, 71
Marlowe, Christopher, 41, 101, 103
   Hero & Leander, 103
   The Jew of Malta, 101
Marot, Clement, 73, 141
Marpa, 65, 68, 138
Martí, José, 55, 91
   Nuestra America, 91
Martin, Fred, 26, 30, 45, 155
Maximus Books, 61
Mayer, Bernadette, 85, 87
McAdams, Lewis, 19
McClure, Michael, 60
   September Blackberries, 60
McCurry, Jim, 17, 21, 28
   Delirium, 28
   Machine, 21, 22, 28
McMahon, Michael, 17, 22, 28
McMonagle, Rik, 58
Melville, Herman, 57, 58
Memphis Minnie (see Douglas, Lizzie), 27
Merchant, Natalie, 118, 119
Meyers, Robert, 6, 39, 45, 62, 139
Micheline, Jack, 52, 137
Mikolowski, Ken, 43, 45, 120, 125
Milarepa, 64, 65, 68, 105, 138
Miles, Steve (photographer and gardener), 118, 128
Miller, Jeffrey, 45
Milton, John
   Paradise Lost, 22, 24
Moe, H. D., 67
Mondrian String Quartet, 57
Money, Peter, 102
Montgomery, David, 20, 22, 23, 29, 32, 46, 50

Morgan, Bill, 118, 129, 134, 139, 145, 146, 155, 156
   Best Minds: A Tribute to Allen Ginsberg (Morgan and Rosenthal, eds.), 134, 156
   I Celebrate Myself: The Somewhat Private Life of Allen Ginsberg, 6, 146, 156
   I Greet You at the Beginning of a Great Career: The Selected Correspondence of Lawrence Ferlinghetti and Allen Ginsberg 1955-1997, 6, 134, 156
   Wait Till I'm Dead: Uncollected Poems, 3, 138, 139, 156
Morganfield, McKinley "Muddy Waters", 27
Murao, Shig, 26
Musaeus, 103
Mussolini, Benito, 102
Myles, Eileen, 81, 142
Nager, Richard, 103
Napalm Health Spa (see Cohn), 99
Naropa (magazine), 62
Naropa Institute (later University), 8, 19, 25, 30, 39, 129, 130, 141
Nashe, Thomas, 24
National Poetry Festival (Allendale, Mi. 1973), 1
Neruda, Pablo, 99
New Blood (magazine), 45, 81
New Directions (publisher), 25, 30, 45, 129, 130, 139, 155
New York Newsday, 104
New York Times, 19, 20, 21, 25, 26, 112
Notley, Alice, 119
O'Hara, Frank, 60, 61, 79
Oppen, George, 1, 18, 48, 49, 50
Oppen, Mary, 48
Oppenheimer, Joel, 56
Orlovsky, Peter, 24, 49, 74, 102, 118, 137, 141
   Clean Asshole Poems and Smiling Vegetable Songs, 49
Owen, Wilfred, 79
Packer, Eve, 106
Palés Matos, Luis, 63
Paragon House, 72
Parkinson, Thomas, 74
   A Casebook on the Beat, 74
Patton, Charlie, 27
Pawelczak, Andy, 76
Pearlman, Al, 43, 46

Pessoa, Fernando, 58, 59, 139
Peters, Robert, 64
Petrarca, Francesco (Petrarch), 65, 141
Petronius, 22
Pingarron, Michael, 80, 81, 103
Pivano, Fernanda, 118
Plato, 100, 104
Poetry, 140
Poetry Flash, 71
Ponderosa Pine (Keith Lampe, environmental activist), 88
Poniewaz, Jeff, 55, 63, 64, 81, 85, 87, 91, 98, 110, 142, 143
Pound, Ezra, 38, 39, 48, 51, 60, 61, 74, 79, 103, 121, 144
 "Letter to William Carlos Williams", 74
 Personae, 48
Prajna Paramita Sutra\, 104
Rainey, Gertrude "Ma", 27
Rakosi, Carl, 1, 17, 24, 72, 74, 92, 127, 141, 155
 Collected Poems, 74
Randall, Dudley, 91
 The Black Poets, 91
Reagan, Ronald, 134
Rexroth, Kenneth, 48, 60, 74
Reznikoff, Charles, 1, 16, 20, 22, 24, 31, 39, 48, 51, 56, 60, 61, 66, 79, 91, 99, 101, 103, 121, 125
 "Depression", 101
 "Kaddish", 135
Rimbaud, Arthur, 22, 54
Rivera, Diego, 31
 The Detroit Industry Murals, 31
Rixon, Bob, 50, 55, 56, 57, 58, 60, 61, 77, 80, 81, 136
 The Strand, 56
Roark, Randy, 53, 56, 129, 139
Roberts, Len, 48
 Cohoes Theater, 48
Rodriguez, Ron, 55
Rolling Stone (magazine), 17, 46
Roof, 29
Rosenthal, Bob, 79, 89, 99, 102, 103, 118, 119, 120, 134, 145, 156
Rosenthal, Irving (editor of *The Chicago Review, Big Table*, etc.), 88

Roskos, Dave, 80
Ross, Charlie, 45, 46
Rothenberg, Jerome
 Shaking the Pumpkin: Traditional Poetry of the Indian North Americas, 99
Rothenberg, Michael, 155
 Big Bridge, 155
Rothschild, Charles, 19, 53
Ruggia, James, 44, 45, 50, 52, 54, 55, 59, 61, 62, 63, 64, 71, 72, 73, 80, 81, 82, 98, 121, 137, 138, 139, 143
Russell, Bertrand, 100
Sakaki, Nanao, 86, 87, 99
San Francisco Chronicle, 74
San Juan de la Cruz, 55
Sanchez, Bertha Bello, 91
Sanders, Ed, 69, 87, 99, 121, 122, 146
Sappho, 41, 104
Schacter-Shalomi, Rabbi Zalman, 119
Schelling, Andrew, 155
Schmidt, Gary and Lin, 38, 133
Schneider, Steve (National Center for Atmospheric Research), 83
Schulman, Grace, 47
Schumacher, Michael, 146, 156
 Dharma Lion: A Critical Biography Of Allen Ginsberg, 6, 146
Sgambati, Al, 44, 55, 81
Shakespeare, William, 1, 2, 22, 24, 27, 41, 62, 65, 91, 98, 101, 102, 107, 111, 137, 141, 144, 157
 As You Like It, 78, 103
 Coriolanus, 102
 Henry IV.1, 22
 Henry V, 102
 Julius Caesar, 102, 103
 King Lear, 22
 Macbeth, 22
 Measure for Measure, 103
 Much Ado About Nothing, 103
 Othello, 91, 102
 Richard II, 102
 Sonnets, 24, 62, 65, 91
 The Comedy of Errors, 101
 The Merchant of Venice, 101
 The Tempest, 31, 78, 91, 98
 Twelfth Night, 78

Shapiro, Harvey, 19, 22, 25
Shapiro, Meyer, 123
Shelley, Percy Byshhe, 24, 41, 52, 82
Sherry, Jim, 29
Sidney, Sir Philip, 41, 141
Silberman, Steve, 76, 77, 92, 98
Skelton, John, 73
Smart, Christopher, 123
Smedman, Lorna, 137
Smith, Bessie, 27
Smith, Patti, 120
Snyder, Gary, 1, 3, 16, 27, 29, 51, 56, 60, 63, 82, 84, 86, 99, 133, 142, 143
   Axe Handles, 60
   The Back Country, 29
Sophocles, 102
   Oedipus Rex, 102
Spenser, Edmund, 24, 41, 141
   The Fairy Queen, 24
St. Christopher, 22
St. Francis of Assisi, 22
Stanbury, Vicki, 76, 82, 90
Steinbeck, IV (Jr.), John, 71, 81, 140
Stieglitz, Alfred, 68
Stutzky, Craig, 106
Suetonius, 42
Sumner, Charles, 38, 134
Swartz, Tom, 41, 44, 45, 46, 51, 52, 55, 62, 81, 137, 139
Tacitus, 42
Taylor, Steven, 57, 69, 78, 79, 121, 140, 141
Tendzin, Ozel, 68
   Buddha in the Palm of Your Hand, 68
The Beat Hotel (film), 134
The Beatles, 57, 105
The Bhagavad Gita, 105
The Clash, 49, 50, 52, 58, 137
The Dalai Lama, 109, 110, 111
The Declaration of Interdependence, 99, 133, 143, 155
The Epic of Gilgamesh, 105
The Fugs, 38, 71, 76, 140
The Golden Ass (Apuleius), 80
The Golden Bough: A Study in Comparative Religion (Sir James Frazer), 80
The Grand Rapids College Review, 89

The Grand Rapids Press, 81, 139
The Heart Sutra, 105
The Kalevala, 132
The Life of Milarepa, 144
The Michigan Daily, 133
The Nation, 47
The Poetry Project Newsletter, 67, 140, 155
The Ramayana, 105
The Rolling Stones, 27
The San Juan Star, 61
The Tibetan Book of the Dead, 21
The White Goddess (Robert Graves), 80
Theocritus, 103, 104
   "Hylas", 103
Thomas, Dylan, 1, 51
Thoreau, Henry David, 58, 85
Time (magazine), 49, 51, 136
Trakl, Georg, 55
Trilling, Lionel, 123
Trotsky, Leon, 123
Trungpa Rinpoche, Chogyam, 57, 64, 68, 72, 74, 106
   Born in Tibet, 57, 68
   Cutting Through Spiritual Materialism, 68, 138
   The Myth of Freedom, 68
Twain, Mark, 54
   Life on the Mississippi, 54
Tysh, George, 59, 60, 61, 139
Udall, Stuart, 87
Vajradhatu Sun, 57
Van Haitsema, Elva, 141
Villon, François, 54, 73, 141
Virgil (Publius Virgilius Maro), 71
   Aeneid, 98
   Eclogues, 71
Waldman, Anne, 9, 11, 19, 67, 82, 83, 85, 86, 87, 95, 115, 119, 127, 144, 146, 155
   "Leir", 102, 103
   De Iovis, 102
Warshall, Peter, 99
Weigl, Bruce, 143
   Song of Napalm, 90, 143
Wells, Ida B., 98
   Crusade for Justice: The Autobiography of Ida B. Wells, 98
Wells, Orson, 102

Whitman, Walt, 23, 25, 27, 29, 85, 91, 101, 107, 108, 109, 121
Williams, William Carlos, 2, 24, 28, 30, 39, 54, 56, 60, 61, 62, 64, 68, 92, 121, 140, 144
Paterson, 22, 28, 30, 68
Wilmarth, Richard, 103
Winters, Greg, 101
Wittgenstein, Ludwig, 100
Wojczuk, Michael, 44
Women's Studies (course at GRCC), 144, 157
Wordsworth, William, 24, 29, 30, 41, 106
"Intimations of Immortality", 24
The Prelude, 30
Writers and Books Newsletter (Rochester, N. Y.), 71
Wyatt, Sir Thomas, 91, 123, 141
Ywahoo, Dhyani, 84
Voices of Our Ancestors: Cherokee Teachings from the Wisdom Fire, 84
Zero, 32, 42
Zhang Ziqing, 3, 139, 157
A History of 20th Century American Poetry (3 vols.) Beijing, 2018, 139, 157
Zivancevic, Nina, 55, 81, 87, 137
Zukofsky, Louis, 39

Related Works

"Allen Ginsberg and David Cope Class on Carl Rakosi." *Naropa University Archives*. June 29, 1987. http://cdm16621.contentdm.oclc.org/cdm/ref/collection/p16621coll1/id/2633

The Allen Ginsberg Papers (finding aid): http://www.oac.cdlib.org/findaid/ark:/13030/tf5c6004hb/

The Allen Ginsberg Homepage: http://allenginsberg.org/#!/

Cope, David. "Crash." *The Pushcart Prize II: Best of the Small Presses*. Ed. Bill Henderson. New York: Avon, 1977.

— Five Poems selected by Allen Ginsberg. *City Lights Journal* #4. Ed. Mendes Monsanto. San Francisco: City Lights, 1978.

— "Marsden Hartley: Forgotten Classic." *The Poetry Project Newsletter* 116. James Ruggia, ed. (November 1985): 1-2.

— Three Poems. *Friction* 5/6: *Obscure Genius*. Ed Allen Ginsberg. Boulder: Laocoon, Winter, 1984. 37-39.

— Two Poems and Fragments. "Ginsberg's Choice." Ed. Allen Ginsberg. *New Directions 37*. Ed. J. Laughlin with Peter Glassgold and Frederick R. Martin. New York: New Directions, 1978.

The David Cope Papers (finding aid): http://quod.lib.umich.edu/s/sclead/umich-scl-cope?subview=standard;view=reslist

The Dave Cope Sampler: http://www.poetspath.com/Dave_Cope/

David Cope Interviewed by Jim Cohn. "Moving On: 41 Years of *Big Scream* / Nada Press." *Big Bridge* 18. Ed Michael Rothenberg.: http://bigbridge.org/BB18/features/BigScream/MOVING_ON.html

"The Declaration of Interdependence." *Disembodied Poetics: Annals of the Jack Kerouac School*. Ed. Anne Waldman and Andrew Schelling.. Albuquerque: U of New Mexico, 1994. 466.
See also page x for acknowledgement of David Cope.

Foreword to *Quiet Lives*. *Deliberate Prose: Selected Essays 1952-1995*. By Allen Ginsberg. Ed. Bill Morgan. New York: HarperCollins, 2000.

Ginsberg, Allen. "Basic Poetics: David Cope." 7 Jan. 1980. Three posts. *The Allen Ginsberg Project*.

       October 12, 2015: http://ginsbergblog.blogspot.com/2015/10/basic-poetics-3-david-cope-1.html

       October 13, 2015: http://ginsbergblog.blogspot.com/2015/10/basic-poetics-4-david-cope-2.html

       October 14, 2015: http://ginsbergblog.blogspot.com/2015/10/basic-poetics-5-david-cope-3.html

—   "Poem." *Wait Till I'm Dead: Uncollected Poems.* Ed. Bill Morgan. New York: Grove, 2016.

—   *Sad Dust Glories: poems during work summer in woods.* Berkeley: The Workingman's Press, 1975.

Morgan, Bill. *I Celebrate Myself: The Somewhat Private Life of Allen Ginsberg.* New York et al: Viking/Penguin, 2006.

—   ed. *I Greet You at the Beginning of a Great Career: The Selected Correspondence of Lawrence Ferlinghetti and Allen Ginsberg 1955-1997.* San Francisco: City Lights, 2015. Pages 235-236, 238, 245-246, 248, 255 [3-in-1 book project].

—   and Bob Rosenthal, eds. *Best Minds: A Tribute to Allen Ginsberg,* New York: Lospecchio, 1986.

Schumacher, Michael. *Dharma Lion: A Critical Biography of Allen Ginsberg.* New York: St. Martin's Press, 1992.

—   Excerpt from Life Events/Chronology for Allen Ginsberg. *The Allen Ginsberg Project:* http://allenginsberg.org/#!/biography Used by permission of Michael Schumacher

About David Cope

Born 1948, Detroit, Mi. Education: BA University of Michigan, MA+30 Western Michigan University. Married 50 years, 3 grown children. Taught Shakespeare, Drama, Creative Writing, Multicultural Literature, Women's Studies, etc. at Grand Rapids Community College for 22 years; school custodian 18 years before that. Kent County Dyer Ives Poetry Competition, first place adult category winner, 1971, 1972. Pushcart Prize winner, 1977. Distinguished Alumni award, GRCC 1984. Nine books and two chapbooks published, winner of award in literature from American Academy/Institute of Arts and Letters, 1988. Editor and publisher, *Big Scream* magazine, 1974-2021. Poet Laureate of Grand Rapids, Mi. 2011-2014; editor of three anthologies: *Nada Poems* (Nada, 1988), *Sunflowers & Locomotives: Songs for Allen* (elegies for Allen Ginsberg, Nada, 1998), and *Song of the Owashtanong: Grand Rapids Poetry in the 21st Century* (Ridgeway, 2013). In 2017, David completed *The Correspondence of David Cope and Allen Ginsberg (1976-1996)*. 2017-2018 publications include *The Train: "Howl" in Chicago* (chapbook, Multifarious Press, 2017), and *The Invisible Keys: New and Selected Poems* 1975-2017 (Ghost Pony Press, 2018). Also in 2018, David's "In Silence" appeared in Chinese translation by Professor Zhang Ziqing as part as group of 9-11 poems in *Houston Garden of Verses*, and nine of his poems were included in translations by Zhang in *Poetry Periodical* (Beijing). In 2019, David's poems were translated and discussed in vol. II (1379-1386) of Professor Zhang's three volume study, *A History of 20th Century American Poetry*. Cope was the only American poet conferee at the Suining International Poetry Week in Sichuan, China (March, 2019). His work from that journey appears in *A Bridge Across the Pacific* (Jabber Publications, 2020). His "River Rouge" appears in *RESPECT: The Poetry of Detroit Music*, ed. Jim Daniels and M. L. Liebler (Michigan State University Press, 2020). The David Cope Papers are maintained at the University of Michigan Special Collections Resource Center, and his webpage, The Dave Cope Sampler, is online at the Museum of American Poetics.

Allen Ginsberg, Adrienne Rich, Sharon Olds and William Stafford paving in garden of poets in Walt Whitman birthplace. Photo by David Cope, 2018.

Printed in Great Britain
by Amazon